PEOPLE YOU
SHOULD KNOW

TOP 101 SCIENTISTS

EDITED BY ELIZABETH LACHNER

Britannica®
Educational Publishing

IN ASSOCIATION WITH

ROSEN
EDUCATIONAL SERVICES

Published in 2017 by Britannica Educational Publishing (a trademark of Encyclopædia Britannica, Inc.) in association with The Rosen Publishing Group, Inc.
29 East 21st Street, New York, NY 10010

Distributed exclusively by Rosen Publishing.
To see additional Britannica Educational Publishing titles, go to rosenpublishing.com.

First Edition

Britannica Educational Publishing
J.E. Luebering: Executive Director, Core Editorial
Anthony L. Green: Editor, Compton's by Britannica

Rosen Publishing
Amelie von Zumbusch: Editor
Nelson Sá: Art Director
Michael Moy: Designer
Cindy Reiman: Photography Manager
Karen Huang: Photo Researcher

Cataloging-in-Publication Data

Names: Lachner, Elizabeth, editor.
Title: Top 101 scientists / edited by Elizabeth Lachner.
Other titles: Top one hundred one scientists | Top one hundred and one
  scientists
Description: First edition. | New York : Britannica Educational Publishing in
  association with Rosen Educational Services, 2017. | 2017 | Series:
  People you should know | Includes bibliographical references and index.
Identifiers: LCCN 2015050941 | ISBN 9781680485103 (library bound : alk. paper)
Subjects: LCSH: Scientists—Biography—Juvenile literature. |
  Science—History—Juvenile literature.
Classification: LCC T39 .T675 2017 | DDC 509.2/2—dc23
LC record available at http://lccn.loc.gov/2015050941

Manufactured in China

Cover (top left) p. 33 © Georgios Kollidas/Fotolia; cover (top center left) p. 60 Kim Shiflett/ NASA; cover (top center right) p. 131 Andrew Toth/Getty Images; cover (right) pp. 25, 41, 79, 98, 101 Photos.com/Thinkstock; cover (bottom left) p. 51 In a private collection; cover (bottom center left) p. 125 Culver Pictures; cover (bottom center right) p. 38 Doris Ullman/Library of Congress, Washington, D.C. (LC-USZC4-4940); cover (bottom right) p. 47 Science Source; pp. vii, 54 ullstein bild/Getty Images; pp. 2, 14, 110 © Encyclopaedia Britannica, Inc.; p. 4 © Argus/Fotolia; p. 9 BBC Hulton Picture Library; p.11 George Grantham Bain Collection/Library of Congress, Washington, D.C. (digital file no. LC-DIG-ggbain-35303); p. 20 Courtesy of the Museum of Jagiellonian University, Kraków, Poland; p. 28 Courtesy of the trustees of the British Museum; photograph, J.R. Freeman & Co. Ltd; p. 43 Cynthia Johnson/The LIFE Images Collection/Getty Images; p. 56 Michael Neugebauer/ The Jane Goodall Institute; p. 69 Staatliche Museen zu Berlin-Preussischer Kulturbesitz; p. 71 Courtesy of the Collection Haags Gemeentemuseum, The Hague; p. 82 AP; p. 85 Courtesy of the Svenska Porträttarkivet, Stockholm; p. 96 Six Great Scientists, by Margaret Avery, 1923; p. 103 Courtesy of the Los Alamos National Laboratory, New Mexico; p. 107 © Library of Congress, Washington, D.C. (cph 3b24095); p. 141 Robert W. Kelley/The LIFE Picture Collection/Getty Images; cover and interior pages border © iStockphoto.com/urbancow

CONTENTS

4

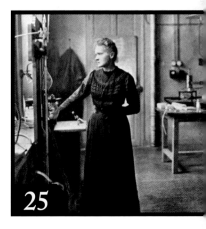

25

38

71

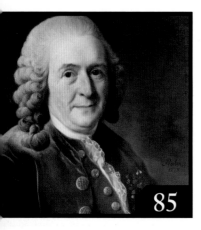

85

98

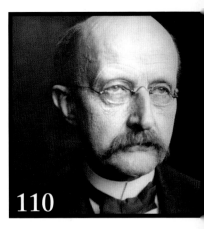

110

125

130

INTRODUCTION

Humans incessantly explore, experiment, create, and examine the world. The active process by which physical, biological, and social phenomena are studied is known as science. Individuals involved in science, called scientists, often spend their entire lives in pursuit of answers to probing questions. This ongoing process often leads to new areas of scientific inquiry.

Although many areas of scientific inquiry are interrelated, specific scientific disciplines, or divisions, have been established. The sciences can be broadly divided into two main areas: the natural sciences and the social sciences. The natural sciences comprise the physical sciences, earth and space sciences, and life sciences; the social sciences encompass disciplines that deal with social and cultural aspects of human behavior, such as economics, sociology, and psychology.

Some scientists are driven by little more than the desire to learn. They may study to gain knowledge for its own sake. These scientists are engaged in basic, or pure, science. Their projects may or may not have any relevance to everyday life. Scientists working in applied science, on the other hand, usually have a specific goal in mind. This goal may involve a product, process, business, or other human need. An applied scientist often uses information recently gathered by other scientists as well as the cumulative knowledge of the pure sciences.

The branches of study that are now called sciences once fell under the heading of philosophy, an umbrella term that suggested the pursuit of knowledge. As recently as the early 19th century, physicists and chemists were still called philosophers. The word "scientist" was invented in 1840 by an English writer, William Whewell. It came gradually to refer to practitioners of a specialized field of knowledge. The prestige of the natural sciences at the time lent its weight to them, in contrast to other branches of study that were not considered to use the scientific method.

The scientific method today is not limited to the methods used in specific branches of science. Every area of study has its own specific goals and its own methods for reaching them. For example, most chemistry

Scientists conduct experiments to learn about the world around them. Here Isaac Newton disperses sunlight through a prism for a study of optics.

research takes place in a lab, while botanical studies may be conducted in greenhouses or in the field. However, the overarching process of the scientific method—forming a hypothesis based on observations of phenomena and using a rigorous approach to investigating that hypothesis—is the foundation of modern research in all areas of science. The goals and methods of research in physics are not the same as those of botany or geology, yet all follow a standard approach to study questions of interest.

Science plays a major role in society, and even nonscientists can appreciate scientific progress. Because of science, human understanding of the past, present, and future is constantly in a state of flux. For instance, decades ago the notion of identifying the entire genetic code of an organism would have seemed an impossible feat. Today it is a mark of scientific progress. Because scientific inquiry never ceases to exist, events once dismissed as material for science fiction, such as medical therapy based on an individual's genetic makeup, now seem inevitable.

LUIS W. ALVAREZ

(b. 1911–d. 1988)

The experimental physicist Luis W. Alvarez won the 1968 Nobel Prize for physics for work that included the discovery of resonance particles—subatomic particles that have very short lifetimes and that occur only in high-energy nuclear collisions. He also worked on the atom bomb in the 1940s. In his later years he theorized that the dinosaurs were made extinct as a result of a meteor crashing into Earth 65 million years ago.

Luis Walter Alvarez was born in San Francisco on June 13, 1911. He was educated at the University of Chicago, where he received a B.S. degree in 1932 and a Ph.D. in 1936. In the latter year he joined the faculty of the University of California at Berkeley, where he became professor of physics in 1945 and later associate director (1954–59, 1975–78) of the Lawrence Radiation Laboratory (now Lawrence Berkeley Laboratory). Alvarez worked on microwave radar research at the Massachusetts Institute of Technology from 1940 to 1943 and at the Los Alamos (New Mexico) Scientific Laboratory from 1944 to 1945. He helped to develop microwave beacons, linear radar antennas, the ground-controlled landing approach system, and a method for aerial bombing that used radar to locate targets. He also suggested the technique for detonating the implosion type of atom bomb.

After World War II Alvarez helped construct the first proton linear accelerator. He also developed the liquid hydrogen bubble chamber in which subatomic particles and their reactions are detected. His autobiography, *Alvarez: Adventures of a Physicist,* was published in 1987. He died in Berkeley on September 1, 1988.

ARCHIMEDES

(b. 287–d. 212 BCE)

The first scientist to recognize and use the power of the lever was Archimedes. This gifted Greek mathematician and inventor once said, "Give me a place to stand and rest my lever on, and I can move the Earth." He also invented the compound pulley and Archimedes's screw. Archimedes was a brilliant mathematician who helped develop the science of geometry. He discovered the relation between the surface area and volume of a sphere and those of its circumscribing cylinder.

A legend says that Archimedes discovered the principle of displacement while stepping into a full bath. He realized that the water that ran over equaled in volume the submerged part of his body. Through further experiments, he deduced the principle of buoyancy, which is called Archimedes's principle. According to this principle a body immersed in a fluid loses as much in weight as the weight of an equal volume of the fluid.

In Archimedes's screw, water or any other liquid is carried up the tube by the turning blade.

Another legend describes how Archimedes uncovered a fraud against King Hieron II of Syracuse using his principle of buoyancy. The king suspected that a solid gold crown he ordered was partly made of silver. Archimedes first took two equal weights of gold and silver and compared their weights when immersed in water. Next he compared the weights of the crown and a pure silver crown of identical dimensions when each was immersed in water. The difference between these two comparisons revealed that the crown was not solid gold.

Archimedes was born in Syracuse, Sicily. He lived there most of his life. When the Romans attacked Syracuse, Archimedes invented weapons to defend the city. He is said to have suggested a method of employing mirrors to set enemy ships afire. After a two-year siege the Romans finally entered the city, and Archimedes was killed in the battle that followed.

ARISTOTLE

(b. 384–d. 322 BCE)

One of the greatest thinkers of all time was Aristotle, an ancient Greek philosopher. His work in the natural and social sciences greatly influenced virtually every area of modern thinking.

Aristotle was born in 384 BCE in Stagira, Chalcidice, Greece, on the northwest coast of the Aegean Sea. His father was a friend and the physician of the king of Macedonia, and he spent most of his boyhood at the court. At 17, he went to Athens to study. He enrolled at the famous Academy directed by the philosopher Plato.

Aristotle threw himself wholeheartedly into Plato's pursuit of truth and goodness. Plato was soon calling him the "mind of the school." Aristotle stayed at the Academy for 20 years, leaving only when his beloved master died in 347 BCE. In later years he renounced some of Plato's theories and went far beyond him in breadth of knowledge.

Aristotle became a teacher in a school on the coast of Asia Minor. He spent two years studying marine biology on Lesbos. In 342 BCE, Philip II invited Aristotle to return to the Macedonian court and teach his

3

Aristotle.

13-year-old son, Alexander. This was the boy who was to become conqueror of the world. No one knows how much influence the philosopher had on the headstrong youth. After Alexander became king, at 20, he gave his teacher a large sum of money to set up a school in Athens, Greece.

In Athens Aristotle taught brilliantly at his school in the Lyceum. He collected the first great library and established a museum. In the mornings he strolled in the Lyceum gardens, discussing problems with his advanced students.

Because he walked about while teaching, Athenians called his school the Peripatetic (which means "to walk about") school. He led his pupils in research in every existing field of knowledge. They dissected animals and studied the habits of insects. The science of observation was new to the Greeks. Hampered by a lack of instruments, they were not always correct in their conclusions.

One of Aristotle's most important contributions was defining and classifying the various branches of knowledge. He sorted them into physics, metaphysics, psychology, rhetoric, poetics, and logic, and thus laid the foundation for most of the sciences of today.

Anti-Macedonian feeling broke out in Athens in 323 BCE. The Athenians accused Aristotle of impiety. He chose to flee so that the Athenians might not "twice sin against philosophy" (by killing him as they had Socrates). He fled to Chalcis on the island of Euboea. There he died the next year.

After his death, Aristotle's writings were scattered or lost. In the early Middle Ages the only works of his known in western Europe were parts of his writings on logic. They became the basis of one of the three subjects of the medieval trivium—logic, grammar, and rhetoric. Early in the 13th century other books reached the West. Some came from Constantinople; others were brought by the Arabs to Spain. Medieval scholars translated them into Latin.

The best known of Aristotle's writings that have been preserved are *Organon* (treatises on logic); *Rhetoric*; *Poetics*; *History of Animals*; *Metaphysics*; *De Anima* (on psychology); *Nicomachean Ethics*; *Politics*; and *Constitution of Athens*. Aristotle died in 322 BCE, in Chalcis, Euboea.

AVICENNA

(b. 980–d. 1037)

During the Middle Ages, few scholars contributed more to science and philosophy than the Muslim scholar Avicenna. By his writings he helped convey the thought of the Greek philosopher Aristotle to the thinkers of western Europe, and his *The Canon of Medicine* became the definitive work in its field for centuries.

Born in Bukhara, Persia (now in Iran), in 980, he spent his childhood and youth studying Islamic law, literature, and medicine. By age 21 he was considered a great scholar and an outstanding physician.

After his father's death, Avicenna left Bukhara and for about twenty years lived in different Persian cities, working as a physician and completing two of his major works. *The Book of Healing* was a large encyclopedia covering the natural sciences, logic, mathematics, psychology, astronomy, music, and philosophy. It is probably the largest work of its kind ever written by one man. *The Canon of Medicine* was a systematic exposition of the achievements of Greek and Roman physicians.

For the last 14 years of his life, Avicenna lived in the city of Isfahan and continued his prodigious writing career. He died in 1037.

In the next century much of Avicenna's work was translated into Latin and thereby became available to the philosophers and theologians of Europe. In Islam his contributions in medicine, theology, and philosophy are still recognized as valuable.

DAVID BALTIMORE

(b. 1938–)

Microbiologist David Baltimore was a leading researcher of viruses and their effect on the development of cancer. Together with Howard M. Temin and Renato Dulbecco, Baltimore shared the Nobel Prize for physiology or medicine in 1975. Working independently, Baltimore and Temin discovered an enzyme that synthesizes DNA from RNA. Baltimore also conducted research that led to an understanding of the interaction between tumor viruses and the genetic material of the cell.

Baltimore was born on March 7, 1938, in New York City. He received a bachelor's degree from Swarthmore College in 1960 and went on to study animal virology at the Rockefeller Institute (now Rockefeller University), where he obtained a doctoral degree in 1964, and at the Massachusetts Institute of Technology (MIT). He became a professor at MIT from 1968 to 1990 but went to Rockefeller from 1990 to 1994, the first two years as president. He was embroiled in a 1991 controversy over a scientific project to which a coworker supposedly added fraudulent data and was asked to resign from Rockefeller. The coworker was subsequently cleared of scientific misconduct charges in 1996. Baltimore returned to MIT from 1994 to 1997, at which time he left to become president of the California Institute of Technology (Caltech) from 1997 to 2006. He was elected president of the American Association for the Advancement of Science in 2006.

DANIEL BERNOULLI

(b. 1700–d. 1782)

The most distinguished member of the second generation of the Bernoulli family of Swiss mathematicians was Daniel Bernoulli. He investigated not only mathematics but also such fields as medicine, biology, physiology, mechanics, physics, astronomy, and oceanography. Bernoulli's theorem, which he derived, is named after him.

Daniel Bernoulli was the second son of Johann Bernoulli, who first taught him mathematics. After studying philosophy, logic, and medicine at the universities of Heidelberg, Strasbourg, and Basel, he received an M.D. degree (1721). In 1723–24 he wrote *Exercitationes quaedam Mathematicae* on differential equations and the physics of flowing water, which won him a position at the influential Academy of Sciences in St. Petersburg, Russia. Bernoulli lectured there until 1732 in medicine, mechanics, and physics, and he researched the properties of vibrating and rotating bodies and contributed to probability theory. In that same year he returned to the University of Basel to accept the post in anatomy and botany. By then he was widely esteemed by scholars and also admired by the public throughout Europe.

Bernoulli's reputation was established in 1738 with *Hydrodynamica*, in which he considered the properties of basic importance in fluid flow, particularly pressure, density, and velocity and set forth their fundamental relationship. He put forward what is called Bernoulli's principle, which states that the pressure in a fluid decreases as its velocity increases. He also established the basis for the kinetic theory of gases and heat by demonstrating that the impact of molecules on a surface would explain pressure and that, assuming the constant, random motion of molecules, pressure and motion increase with temperature. About 1738 his father published *Hydraulica*; this attempt by Johann Bernoulli to obtain priority for himself showed his antagonism toward his son.

Between 1725 and 1749 Daniel won 10 prizes from the Paris Academy of Sciences for work on astronomy, gravity, tides, magnetism, ocean currents, and the behavior of ships at sea. He also made substantial contributions in probability. He shared the 1735 prize for work on planetary orbits with his father, who, it is said, threw him out of the house for obtaining a prize he felt should have been his alone. Daniel's accolades reflected his success on the research frontiers of science and his ability to set forth clearly before an interested public the scientific problems of the day. In 1732 he accepted a post in botany and anatomy at Basel; in 1743, one in physiology; and in 1750, one in physics.

JOSEPH BLACK

(b. 1728–d. 1799)

The British chemist and physicist Joseph Black is best known for the rediscovery of "fixed air" (carbon dioxide), the concept of latent heat, and the discovery of the bicarbonates (such as bicarbonate of soda). Born April 16, 1728, Black was the son of expatriate Ulster merchant

John Black and his wife, Margaret Gordon. He studied medicine at both the University of Glasgow and University of Edinburgh, from which he earned a medical degree in 1754. As part of his thesis, he conducted a series of experiments on the chemical properties of an alkali—in particular, magnesia alba, now known as magnesium carbonate. These laid the basis for the most important paper of his career, *Experiments upon Magnesia Alba, Quicklime, and Some Other Alcaline Substances*, given to the Philosophical Society of Edinburgh in 1755. He found that with acids, magnesia alba behaved in a similar way

Joseph Black.

to chalk (calcium carbonate), giving off a gas. He then heated a sample of the starting compound and found that the product, magnesia usta (now known as magnesium oxide), like quicklime (calcium oxide), did not effervesce with acids. Unlike quicklime, however, it was not caustic or soluble in water. Black hypothesized that the weight lost during heating was due to the gas generated. He then added a solution of potash (potassium carbonate) to the magnesia usta and showed that the product weighed the same as his original sample of magnesia alba. The difference between the alba and usta was therefore the gas, which Black called fixed air. It could be introduced to the latter to re-create the former by means of the potash.

Black broadened his experiments and took his conclusions to a higher stage in his 1756 paper to the Philosophical Society. He concentrated on calcium rather than magnesium salts, showing that, when chalk is heated strongly to quicklime, a gas is given off, and he concluded that this gas derives from the chalk and not from the fire in the furnace; this had been a point of contention among Edinburgh professors. The gas could be replaced by adding potash solution to the quicklime, which demonstrated that the fixed air is contained in the alkali. Black then showed that the gas is not a version of atmospheric air. He was the first chemist to show that gases could be chemical substances in themselves and not, as had been thought beforehand, atmospheric air in different states of purity.

NIELS BOHR

(b. 1885–d. 1962)

One of the foremost scientists of the 20th century, the Nobel Prize-winning physicist Niels Bohr was the first to apply the quantum theory to atomic structure. His interpretation of the meaning of quantum physics was to become a basic tenet of the science.

Niels Henrik David Bohr was born in Copenhagen, Denmark, on October 7, 1885. His father was a professor of physiology at the University of Copenhagen, and young Bohr grew up among scientists. He entered the university in 1903, winning in 1907 the gold medal of the Royal Danish Academy of Sciences and Letters for his experiments with the vibrations of water to determine its surface tensions.

In 1911 Bohr went to England to study with J. J. Thomson and Ernest Rutherford. His first great work began with a study of the theoretical implications of the nuclear model of the atom proposed by Rutherford. In 1913 he combined the concept of the nuclear atom with the quantum theory of Max Planck and Albert Einstein, departing radically from classical physics. He returned to Copenhagen in 1916 as a professor at the university, becoming director in 1920 of the university's Institute for Theoretical Physics, to which he attracted world-renowned physicists. In 1922 he won the Nobel Prize for Physics for his work on atomic structure.

Niels Bohr.

When Bohr visited the United States early in 1939, he brought with him the knowledge that German scientists had succeeded in splitting the uranium atom. Bohr worked during the winter of 1939–40 at Princeton University, where he developed the theory of atomic fission that led directly to the first atomic bomb. He returned to Denmark in 1940.

After the Germans occupied his country, Bohr was active in the anti-Nazi resistance movement. Under threat of arrest because of his Jewish ancestry, he escaped by fishing boat to Sweden in 1943. He was then flown secretly to England. In the United States he was an adviser on the atomic bomb project but did not remain to see the first test bomb exploded. In 1957 he received the first United States Atoms for Peace Award. He died in Copenhagen on November 18, 1962. Bohr's essays were collected in *Atomic Theory and the Description of Nature* (1934); *Atomic Physics and Human Knowledge* (1958); and *Essays, 1958–1962, on Atomic Physics and Human Knowledge* (1963). His son, Aage Bohr, was a joint winner of the Nobel Prize in Physics in 1975 for his own work on atomic structure.

MAX BORN

(b. 1882–d. 1970)

Born in Breslau, Germany, the British physicist Max Born taught and conducted research at several German universities before he was forced to emigrate in 1933. He became a British subject in 1939. Born was Tait professor of natural philosophy at the University of Edinburgh from 1936 to 1953, when he retired and moved to West Germany. In 1954, he was corecipient of the Nobel Prize in physics for the statistical description of the behavior of subatomic particles. Born was an early leader in explaining wave-particle ambiguities of physics and helped formulate quantum theory. He also introduced the Born approximation for solving problems concerning the scattering of atomic particles. After his retirement, he continued to write on scientific issues and coauthored *Principles of Optics* (1959).

ROBERT BOYLE

(b. 1627–d. 1691)

R obert Boyle was a preeminent figure of 17th-century intellectual culture. He was best known as a natural philosopher, particularly in the field of chemistry, but his scientific work covered many areas, including hydrostatics, physics, medicine, earth sciences, natural history, and alchemy. His prolific output also included Christian devotional and ethical essays and theological tracts. In 1660 he helped found the Royal Society of London.

Boyle was born into one of the wealthiest families in Britain on January 25, 1627. He was the 14th child and 7th son of Richard Boyle, the 1st earl of Cork, by his second wife, Catherine, daughter of Sir Geoffrey Fenton, secretary of state for Ireland.

In 1654 Boyle was invited to Oxford, and he took up residence at the university from c. 1656 until 1668. In Oxford he was exposed to the latest developments in natural philosophy and became associated with a group of notable natural philosophers and physicians, including John Wilkins, Christopher Wren, and John Locke. These individuals, together with a few others, formed the Experimental Philosophy Club, which at times met in Boyle's lodgings. Much of Boyle's best-known work dates from this period. In 1659 he and Robert Hooke completed the construction of their famous air pump and used it to study pneumatics. Their resultant discoveries regarding air pressure and the vacuum appeared in Boyle's first scientific publication, *New Experiments Physico-Mechanicall, Touching the Spring of the Air and Its Effects* (1660). Boyle and Hooke discovered several physical characteristics of air, including its role in combustion, respiration, and the transmission of sound. One of their findings, published in 1662, later became known as Boyle's law. This law expresses the inverse relationship that exists between the pressure and volume of a gas, and it was determined by measuring the volume occupied by a constant quantity of air when compressed by differing weights of mercury.

Boyle's scientific work is characterized by its reliance on experiment and observation and its reluctance to formulate generalized theories. He advocated a "mechanical philosophy" that saw the universe as a huge machine or clock in which all natural phenomena were accountable purely by mechanical, clockwork motion. His contributions to chemistry were based on a mechanical "corpuscularian hypothesis"— a brand of atomism which claimed that everything was composed of minute (but not indivisible) particles of a single universal matter and

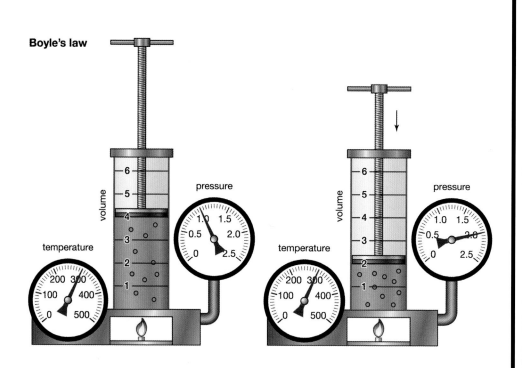

Boyle's law

Demonstration of Boyle's law showing that for a given mass, at constant temperature, the pressure times the volume is a constant.

that these particles were only differentiable by their shape and motion. Among his most influential writings were *The Sceptical Chymist* (1661), which assailed the then-current notions about the composition of matter and methods of chemical analysis, and the *Origine of Formes and Qualities* (1666), which used chemical phenomena to support the corpuscularian hypothesis. Boyle also maintained a lifelong pursuit of alchemy, hoping to discover the secret of transmuting base metals into gold. Overall, Boyle argued so strongly for the need of applying the principles and methods of chemistry to the study of the natural world and to medicine that he later became known as the father of chemistry.

ROBERT BROWN

(b. 1773–d. 1858)

Scottish botanist Robert Brown is best known for his descriptions of cell nuclei and the continuous motion of minute particles in solution, which came to be called Brownian motion. In addition, he recognized the fundamental distinction between gymnosperms (conifers and their allies) and angiosperms (flowering plants), and he improved plant taxonomy by establishing and defining new families and genera. He contributed substantially to the knowledge of plant morphology, embryology, and biogeography, in particular by his original work on the flora of Australia.

Brown was the son of a Scottish Episcopalian clergyman. He studied medicine at the Universities of Aberdeen and Edinburgh. A visit to London in 1798 brought Brown to the notice of Sir Joseph Banks, president of the Royal Society. Banks recommended Brown to the Admiralty for the post of naturalist aboard a ship, the *Investigator*, for a surveying voyage along the northern and southern coasts of Australia. Brown sailed with the expedition in July 1801. While the ship circumnavigated Australia, Brown made extensive plant collections. The results of Brown's Australian trip were partially published in 1810 in *Prodromus Florae Novae Hollandiae et Insulae Van Diemen*, a classic of systematic botany and his major work.

In 1828 Brown published a pamphlet, *A Brief Account of Microscopical Observations...*, about his observations of the "rapid oscillatory motion" of a variety of microscopic particles. He recorded that, after noticing moving particles (now known to be amyloplasts, organelles involved with starch synthesis) suspended within living pollen grains of *Clarkia pulchella*, he examined both living and dead pollen grains of many other plants and observed a similar motion in all of them. Brown then experimented with organic and inorganic substances reduced to a fine powder and suspended in water. His work revealed the random movement to be a general property of matter in that state, and the phenomenon has long been known as Brownian motion in his honor.

In 1831, while investigating the fertilization mechanisms of plants in the *Orchidaceae* and *Asclepiadaceae* families, Brown noted the existence of a structure within the cells of orchids, as well as many other plants, that he termed the "nucleus" of the cell. Although Brown's were not the first observations of cell nuclei, his designation of the term has persisted.

HENRY CAVENDISH

(b. 1731–d. 1810)

E nglish chemist and physicist Henry Cavendish was distinguished for the great accuracy and precision of his scientific research. He was especially noted for his experiment to determine the weight of the Earth, which has come to be known as the Cavendish experiment.

Cavendish was born on October 10, 1731, in Nice, France. In England he studied for several years at Cambridge University and then settled in London, where he set up his own laboratory and dedicated his life to science. By 1766 Cavendish had produced "inflammable air" (hydrogen) by dissolving metals in acids and "fixed air" (carbon dioxide) by dissolving alkalis in acids; he collected these and other gases in bottles inverted over water or mercury. He then measured their solubility in water and their specific gravity and noted their combustibility. For this work, Cavendish was awarded the Copley Medal, given annually by the Royal Society of London "for outstanding achievements in research in any branch of science." In addition, Cavendish later developed a general theory of heat and discovered various properties of electricity.

In 1798 Cavendish carried out his most famous experiment. To determine the density of the Earth, he modified an apparatus built by fellow Englishman geologist John Michell, who had died in 1793. The apparatus employed was a torsion balance, essentially a stretched wire supporting spherical weights. Cavendish measured the force of gravitational attraction between pairs of lead spheres, which allowed the first calculation of the value of the gravitational constant, G. The determination of G permitted calculation of the Earth's density, and the result that Cavendish obtained is within 1 percent of the currently accepted figure.

Cavendish died on February 24, 1810, in London. A collection of his manuscripts, *The Scientific Papers of the Honourable Henry Cavendish, F.R.S.*, appeared in 1921.

ARTHUR HOLLY COMPTON

(b. 1892–d. 1962)

The scientist who first described the behavior of X-rays when they interact with electrons was the American physicist Arthur Holly Compton. In his early research on the measurement of radiation, he found that when X-rays strike graphite they are scattered and their wavelengths are increased. This discovery—known as the Compton effect—was the first proof that X-rays can act like particles. This discovery was significant because it confirmed the theory that electromagnetic radiation can act as both a wave and a particle.

Arthur Holly Compton was born in Wooster, Ohio, on September 10, 1892. He was the youngest son of Elias and Otelia Augspurger Compton, who had two other sons and a daughter. Compton first became interested in science, chiefly in the fields of aviation and astronomy, as a child. During his first years of amateur astronomy he photographed constellations and Halley's comet through a telescope he purchased. Later he constructed and flew a glider with a wingspan of 27 feet (8 meters).

In 1913 he graduated from the College of Wooster. At Princeton University he earned a master's degree in physics in 1914 and a doctorate in 1916. After completing his studies, he married Betty McCloskey. They had two sons. Compton's teaching career began in 1916 at the University of Minnesota. During World War I he helped develop airplane instruments. In 1919 he went to Cambridge University in England on a one-year fellowship grant.

After three years as head of the physics department at Washington University, in St. Louis, Missouri, Compton joined the faculty of the University of Chicago in 1923. For his discovery there of the Compton effect, he shared the 1927 Nobel Prize in physics with C. T. R. Wilson, a Scottish physicist. Compton also demonstrated the total reflection of X-rays and collaborated in the polarization of X-rays. Investigating cosmic rays, he discovered their electrical composition. From 1931 to 1933 he directed a world cosmic-ray survey.

During World War II, Compton headed the early phase of the Manhattan District, formed by the United States Army Corps of Engineers to develop the atomic bomb. As director of the project's Metallurgical Laboratory at the University of Chicago, he was in charge of the development of the first nuclear chain reaction, paving the way for the controlled release of nuclear energy. Between 1942 and 1945 he also directed the government's plutonium-research project. He was the governor of the Argonne National Laboratory in 1945.

Compton was appointed chancellor of Washington University in 1945 and was professor of natural philosophy there from 1953 to 1961. He died in Berkeley, California, on March 15, 1962.

NICOLAUS COPERNICUS

(b. 1473–d. 1543)

The Polish astronomer Nicolaus Copernicus is often considered the founder of modern astronomy. His study led to his theory that Earth and the other planets revolve around the Sun.

Copernicus was born on February 19, 1473, in Torun, Poland. His father was a well-to-do merchant, and his mother also came from a leading merchant family. After his father's death, the boy was reared by his uncle, a wealthy Catholic bishop, who sent him to the University of Kraków. There he studied liberal arts, including astronomy and astrology. Copernicus also studied law at Bologna and medicine at Padua in Italy. Following his studies, he became an officer in the Roman Catholic Church. In 1500 he lectured on mathematical subjects in Rome. He returned to his uncle's castle near Frauenburg in 1507 as attending physician to the elderly man. Copernicus spent his spare time studying the heavens.

For centuries before Copernicus's time, astronomy had been based on Ptolemy's theory that Earth was the center of the universe and motionless. The problem was to explain how the other planets and heavenly bodies moved. At first it was thought that they simply moved in circular orbits around Earth. Calculations based on this view, however, did not agree with actual observations. Then it was thought that the other planets traveled in small circular orbits. These in turn were believed to move along larger orbits around Earth. With this theory, however, it could not be proved that Earth was the center of the universe.

Copernicus's revolutionary idea was that Earth should be regarded as one of the planets that revolved around the Sun. He also stated that Earth rotated on an axis. Copernicus, however, still clung to the ideas of planets traveling in small circular orbits that moved along larger orbits.

Copernicus probably hit upon his main idea sometime between 1508 and 1514. For years, however, he delayed publication of his controversial work, which contradicted all the authorities of the time. The historic book that contains the final version of his theory, *De revolutionibus orbium*

Nicolaus Copernicus.

coelestium libri vi (*Six Books Concerning the Revolutions of the Heavenly Orbs*), did not appear in print until 1543, the year of his death. According to legend, Copernicus received a copy as he was dying, on May 24, 1543. The book opened the way to a truly scientific approach to astronomy. It had a profound influence on later thinkers of the scientific revolution, including such major figures as Galileo, Johannes Kepler, and Isaac Newton.

FRANCIS CRICK

(b. 1916–d. 2004)

B ritish biochemist Francis Crick helped make one of the most important discoveries of 20th-century biology—the determination of the molecular structure of deoxyribonucleic acid (DNA). For this accomplishment, Crick received, with colleagues James D. Watson and Maurice Wilkins, the 1962 Nobel Prize for physiology or medicine.

Francis Harry Compton Crick was born on June 8, 1916, in Northampton, Northamptonshire, England. He was educated at University College, London. During World War II, he helped develop magnetic mines for naval use, and from 1949 to 1977 he was on the staff of Cambridge University's Cavendish Laboratories.

In 1951, when Watson arrived at Cambridge, it was known that the mysterious nucleic acids, especially DNA, played a central role in the hereditary determination of the structure and function of each cell. Watson convinced Crick that knowledge of DNA's three-dimensional structure would make its hereditary role apparent. Using X-ray diffraction studies of DNA done by Wilkins, Watson and Crick were able to construct a molecular model consistent with the known physical and chemical properties of DNA. The model consisted of two intertwined helical (spiral) strands of sugar-phosphate, bridged horizontally by flat organic bases.

Crick later discovered that each group of three bases (a codon) on a single DNA strand designates the position of a specific amino acid on the backbone of a protein molecule. He also helped determine which codons code for each amino acid normally found in protein, thus clarifying the way the cell uses DNA to build proteins.

Crick was elected to the U.S. National Academy of Sciences in 1969. From 1977 he held the position of distinguished professor at the Salk Institute for Biological Studies in San Diego, California. He published a number of books, including *Of Molecules and Men* (1966), *What Mad Pursuit: A Personal View of Scientific Discovery* (1988), and *The Astonishing Hypothesis* (1994). He was awarded the Order of Merit in 1991. Crick died on July 28, 2004, in San Diego.

MARIE CURIE

(b. 1867–d. 1934)

Polish-born French physicist Marie Curie was famous for her work on radioactivity and twice a winner of the Nobel Prize. With Henri Becquerel and her husband, Pierre Curie, she was awarded the 1903 Nobel Prize for Physics. She was the sole winner of the 1911 Nobel Prize for Chemistry. Marie Curie was the first woman to win a Nobel Prize, and she is the only woman to win the award in two different fields.

Maria Salomea Sklodowska was born on November 7, 1867, in Warsaw, in what was then the Congress Kingdom of Poland, Russian Empire. From childhood she was remarkable for her prodigious memory, and at the age of 16 she won a gold medal on completion of her secondary education at the Russian lycée. Because her father, a teacher of mathematics and physics, lost his savings through a bad investment, she had to take work as a teacher and at the same time took part clandestinely in the nationalist "free university," reading in Polish to women workers. At the age of 18 she took a post as a governess, where she suffered an unhappy love affair. However, from her earnings she was able to finance her sister Bronislawa's medical studies in Paris, France, with the understanding that Bronislawa would in turn later help her to get an education.

In 1891 Sklodowska went to Paris and—now using the name Marie— began to follow the lectures of Paul Appel, Gabriel Lippmann, and Edmond Bouty at the Sorbonne. Sklodowska worked far into the night and completed degrees in physics and math. It was in the spring of 1891 that she met Pierre Curie.

Their marriage (July 25, 1895) marked the start of a partnership that was soon to achieve results of world significance, in particular the discovery of polonium (so called by Marie in honor of her native land) in the summer of 1898 and that of radium a few months later. Following Henri Becquerel's discovery (1896) of a new phenomenon (which she later called radioactivity), Marie Curie, looking for a subject for a thesis, decided to find out if the property discovered in uranium was to be found in other matter. She discovered that this was true for thorium at the same time as Gerhard Carl Schmidt did.

Turning her attention to minerals, she found her interest drawn to pitchblende. Pitchblende, a mineral whose activity is superior to that of pure uranium, could be explained only by the presence in the ore of small quantities of an unknown substance of very high activity. Pierre Curie then joined Marie in the work that she had undertaken to resolve this problem and that led to the discovery of the new elements, polonium and radium. While Pierre Curie devoted himself chiefly to the physical study of the new radiations, Marie Curie struggled to obtain pure radium in the metallic state—achieved with the help of the chemist André-Louis Debierne, one of Pierre Curie's pupils. On the results of this research, Marie Curie received her doctorate of science in June 1903 and—with Pierre—was awarded the Davy Medal of the Royal Society. Also in 1903 they shared with Becquerel the Nobel Prize for Physics for the discovery of radioactivity.

The birth of her two daughters, Irène and Ève, in 1897 and 1904 did not interrupt Marie's intensive scientific work. She was appointed lecturer in physics (1900) at the École Normale Supérieure for girls in Sèvres, France, and introduced there a method of teaching based on experimental demonstrations. In December 1904 she was appointed chief assistant in the laboratory directed by Pierre Curie.

The sudden death of Pierre Curie (April 19, 1906) was a bitter blow to Marie Curie, but it was also a decisive turning point in her career: henceforth she was to devote all her energy to completing alone the scientific work that they had undertaken. On May 13, 1906, she was appointed to the professorship that had been left vacant on her husband's death; she was the first woman to teach in the Sorbonne. In 1908 she became titular professor, and in 1910 her fundamental treatise on radioactivity was published. In 1911 she was awarded the Nobel Prize for chemistry, for the isolation of pure radium. In 1914 she saw the completion of the building of the laboratories of the Radium Institute (Institut du Radium) at the University of Paris.

Throughout World War I, Marie Curie, with the help of her daughter Irène, devoted herself to the development of the use of X-radiography. In 1918 the Radium Institute, the staff of which Irène had joined, began to operate in earnest, and it was to become a universal center for nuclear physics and chemistry. Marie Curie, now at the highest point of her fame and, from 1922, a member of the Academy of Medicine, devoted her researches to the study of the chemistry of radioactive substances and the medical applications of these substances.

In 1921, accompanied by her two daughters, Marie Curie made a triumphant journey to the United States, where President Warren G. Harding presented her with a gram of radium that had been bought as the result of a collection among American women. Curie gave lectures, especially in Belgium, Brazil, Spain, and Czechoslovakia. She was made a member of the International Commission on Intellectual Co-operation by the Council of the League of Nations. In addition, she had the satisfaction of seeing the development of the Curie Foundation in Paris and in Poland the inauguration in 1932 in Warsaw of the Radium Institute, of which her sister Bronislawa became director.

One of Marie Curie's outstanding achievements was to have understood the need to accumulate intense radioactive sources, not only to treat illness but also to maintain an abundant supply for research in nuclear physics; the resultant stockpile was an unrivaled instrument until the appearance after 1930 of particle accelerators. The existence in Paris at the Radium Institute of a stock of 1.5 grams of radium in which, over a period of several years, radium D and polonium had accumulated made a decisive contribution to the success of the experiments undertaken in the years around 1930 — in particular of those experiments performed by Irène Curie in conjunction with Frédéric Joliot, whom she had married in 1926. This work prepared the way for the discovery of the neutron by Sir James Chadwick and, above all, for the discovery in 1934 by Irène and Frédéric Joliot-Curie of artificial radioactivity. A few months after this discovery, Marie Curie died as a result of leukemia caused by the action of radiation. Her contribution to physics had been immense, not only in

Marie Curie.

her own work, the importance of which had been demonstrated by the award to her of two Nobel Prizes, but because of her influence on subsequent generations of nuclear physicists and chemists.

Marie Curie died on July 4, 1934, near Sallanches, France. In 1995 her ashes were enshrined in the Panthéon in Paris. She was the first woman to receive this honor for her own achievements. Her office and laboratory in the Curie Pavilion of the Radium Institute are preserved as the Curie Museum.

GEORGES CUVIER

(b. 1769–d. 1832)

During the troubled days of the French Revolution and the Napoleonic era, Georges Cuvier was laying the foundations of the science of comparative anatomy. This science studies the structure of animals of various groups to discover their relationships.

Cuvier was so curious about the structure of animals that he dissected, or cut open and examined, specimens from every important group in the animal kingdom. From the time of Carolus Linnaeus, animals had been classified by their outward appearance. Cuvier found, however, that some so-called higher animals are less highly developed than some that were placed low in the "scale of being." He therefore reclassified animals on the basis of their internal structure.

Another of Cuvier's great contributions was the principle of "correlation of parts." In this principle Cuvier stated that the parts of an animal are so closely related that a change in one part may involve a change in another. For example, in developing teeth for biting off and chewing grass, cattle and other ruminants also developed a special form of stomach for digesting grass. But the flesh-tearing teeth of a tiger are associated with a stomach that digests flesh.

Georges Cuvier was born on August 23, 1769, in Montbéliard, France. He showed a special liking for natural history early in life. While he was a student at the Carolinian Academy at Stuttgart (Germany), he read nearly all of the scientific books in the library and learned how to dissect animals. From 1788 to 1794 he studied marine animals. During these years he was tutor with a family living in Normandy, France. Here he met the Abbé Tessier, a keen student of natural history, who urged the young Cuvier to go to Paris and seek greater opportunities.

In Paris Cuvier rose rapidly to fame. He was made assistant professor of comparative anatomy at the Jardin des Plantes in 1795 and full professor in 1802. From 1800 to 1805 he issued, in five volumes, his famous treatise on comparative anatomy, the first treatise to systematize this study. His work on the fossil bones of quadrupeds (1812) established the science of vertebrate paleontology. In 1816 he issued his greatest book— *The Animal Kingdom Arranged According to Its Organization*. In 1818 he was elected to the French Academy.

Napoleon appointed Cuvier inspector of education in 1802, a council member of the Imperial University in 1808, and a councilor of state in 1814. He was made an officer of the Legion of Honor in 1826 and a baron in 1831. He died in Paris on May 13, 1832.

JOHN DALTON

(b. 1766–d. 1844)

English meteorologist and chemist John Dalton was a pioneer in the development of modern atomic theory. Because of his scientific contributions, he is at times considered both the father of chemistry and the father of meteorology.

Dalton was born on September 5 or 6, 1766, in Eaglesfield, Cumberland, England, into a Quaker family of tradesmen. He attended John Fletcher's Quaker grammar school in Eaglesfield. His older brother took over the school when Dalton was 12 years old and had him assist with teaching. Two years later the brothers purchased a school in Kendal, where they taught approximately 60 students. Dalton's mentors, Elihu Robinson and John Gough, taught him the rudiments of mathematics, Greek, and Latin. From them Dalton also gained knowledge in the construction and use of meteorologic instruments as well as instruction in keeping daily weather records.

John Dalton.

In 1793 Dalton moved to Manchester to teach mathematics at the New College. He took with him the proof sheets of his first book, a collection of essays on meteorologic topics based on his own observations together with those of his friends Gough and Peter Crosthwaite. This work, *Meteorological Observations and Essays*, was published in 1793. It contained original ideas that, together with Dalton's more developed articles, marked the transition of meteorology from a topic of general folklore to a serious scientific pursuit.

Soon after his arrival at Manchester, Dalton was elected a member of the Manchester Literary and Philosophical Society. His first contribution to this society was a description of the defect he had discovered in his own and his brother's vision. This paper was the first publication on color blindness, which for some time thereafter was known as Daltonism.

Dalton's most influential work in chemistry was his atomic theory, published in 1808. This theory states, among other things, that each chemical element has atoms that vary in shape and size (in contrast to earlier ideas that all atoms are essentially alike).

Dalton's atomic theory eventually began to win praise, and its author gained widespread recognition. He was elected into the fellowship of the Royal Society of London and the Royal Society of Edinburgh, awarded an honorary degree from the University of Oxford, and elected as one of only eight foreign associates of the French Academy of Sciences. In Manchester he was elected president of the Literary and Philosophical Society in 1817; he held that office for the rest of his life. The society provided him with a laboratory after the New College moved to York. Dalton remained in Manchester and taught private pupils. He died there of a stroke on July 27, 1844, and was given the equivalent of a state funeral by his fellow townspeople.

CHARLES DARWIN

(b. 1809–d. 1882)

The theory of evolution by natural selection that was developed by Charles Darwin revolutionized the study of living things. In his *Origin of Species* (1859) he provided a scientific explanation of how the diverse species of plants and animals have descended over time from common ancestors. His theory remains central to the foundations of modern biology. Moreover, by demonstrating how natural laws govern the world of living things, Darwin helped usher in a new era in the cultural and intellectual history of humankind.

Charles Robert Darwin was born in Shrewsbury, England, on February 12, 1809. Darwin's father was a successful and wealthy physician; his mother was a daughter of Josiah Wedgwood, the famous British potter. She died when Charles was eight years old, and the boy was reared by three older sisters, who constantly found fault with him.

At the age of 16, Darwin began to study medicine at the University of Edinburgh. There too he found the courses dull, and watching operations made him ill. In 1828 he transferred to Cambridge, intending to become a clergyman. Instead, he devoted most of his time to studying plants and animals and later to geology. He received his bachelor's degree in 1831.

Then came the event that shaped his life—an appointment as unpaid naturalist on the exploring ship *Beagle*. It left England on December 27, 1831, to chart the southern coasts of South America and sail around the world. The voyage, with many side trips on land, lasted until October 1836. During those five years Darwin examined geologic formations, collected fossils, and studied plants and animals. In the jungles, mountains, and islands he visited, he saw evidence of the many geologic changes that have been occurring over the course of eons—for example, the land gradually rising in some places and falling in others. He also considered the great diversity of living things, even in the depths of the ocean where no humans could appreciate their beauty. He thought about how the fossils he collected suggested that some kinds of mammals had died out. And he returned home filled with questions.

Back home, Darwin settled in London and quietly began work on what would become his great theory of evolution, developed largely in 1837–39. Meanwhile, he wrote up the journal of his scientific work on the *Beagle* for publication. He also consulted experts to help him identify the thousands of fossils and specimens he had brought back, and he published the results. In 1839 he was admitted to the prestigious Royal Society.

Darwin married his cousin Emma Wedgwood in 1839, and they eventually had 10 children. He began to avoid society, and in 1842 the couple moved to the isolated village of Downe. This was partly owing to physical illness: a few years earlier, Darwin had begun to experience the heart palpitations and nausea that would plague him for the rest of his life. But he also sought seclusion because he knew that his radical theory would shock and offend Victorian society. Believing in evolution, Darwin said, was "like confessing a murder." And so he continued this work in secret.

In Darwin's time, the nearly universally accepted view was that God had created all species of living things in their current forms and that their attributes were the result of God's design. Nevertheless, Darwin was not the first to suggest that living things might change over time. Since ancient times, people have proposed other ways that plants and animals could have developed. The first broad theory of evolution was proposed in the early 19th century by French naturalist Jean-Baptiste Lamarck. He maintained that plants and animals evolved because of an inborn tendency to progress from simple to complex forms. Environment, however, modified this progression and so did use or disuse of parts. He thought that giraffes, for example, developed long necks by straining to reach the leaves of trees, while snakes lost their legs by crawling.

Darwin knew about Lamarck's theory of evolution. His grandfather, Erasmus Darwin, had published several books expounding similar ideas. He felt, however, that early writers on the subject had speculated too much and had not based their theories on a solid foundation of observable phenomena. In developing his theory of evolution, Darwin drew upon observations made in a wide array of scientific disciplines and conducted a great many experiments.

Darwin also happened to read *An Essay on the Principle of Population*, by British economist Thomas Malthus. Malthus had undertaken to prove that human populations tend to increase more rapidly than food and other necessities. The result is a struggle in which some people succeed and become wealthy while others fail or even starve.

Darwin applied this theory to the world of nature. Plants and animals, he knew, reproduce so rapidly that the Earth could not hold them if all their young survived. This meant that there was a constant struggle for space, food, and shelter, as well as against enemies and unfavorable conditions.

Certain hawks, for example, struggle, or compete, with each other for the mice they eat, and the poorest hunters go hungry. Mice, in turn, struggle to keep from being caught by hawks. In frigid winters living things struggle against the cold. Some endure it, while others fail to keep themselves warm enough and die. Although Darwin did not coin the phrase "survival of the fittest," his ideas about struggle expressed the same notion.

Struggling and living or dying could not lead to evolution if all members of each living kind or species were exactly alike. Darwin found that members of a single species vary greatly in shape, size, color, strength, and so on. He also believed that most of these variations could be inherited.

Under the constant struggle to exist, organisms with harmful variations are more likely to die before they can reproduce. And, on average, living things with useful variations are more likely to survive and bear young and thus to pass on their helpful variations. When their descendants vary still more, the process is repeated. In other words, the struggle for existence selects organisms with helpful variations but makes others die out. Darwin called this process natural selection.

Over the ages, Darwin believed, changes from natural selection produce a slow succession of new plants, animals, and other organisms. These changes have enabled living things to go into all sorts of environments and become fitted, or adapted, to many different types of life. Darwin called his theory descent by modification because he proposed that all living things were descended from earlier forms.

Darwin wrote a short sketch of his theory in 1842 and a longer one in 1844. Instead of publishing the second statement, however, he continued his investigations. He also wrote books on coral reefs, volcanic islands, barnacles, and the geology of South America. Not until 1856 did he begin what would be a multivolume work on evolution.

In 1858 he received a manuscript from a young naturalist, Alfred Russel Wallace, who also had developed a theory of evolution by natural selection. With Wallace's approval, short statements by both men were published late in 1858. Darwin went on to write his famous book *On the Origin of Species by Means of Natural Selection*, which appeared in 1859.

The book caused a tremendous stir, and not just in scientific circles. The general public also read, discussed, and vigorously defended or denounced Darwin's theory, which became a popular topic in society

Charles Darwin.

salons. Some religious leaders believed that evolution was incompatible with their teachings and so opposed it. Newspapers publicized with great scorn a conclusion that Darwin had been careful to avoid—that humans are descended from apes. Evolutionary imagery spread through many other fields, including literature, economics, and political and social science. During Darwin's lifetime, the scientific community largely accepted his theory of descent, though it was slower to adopt his idea of natural selection.

After completing the *Origin of Species*, Darwin began *The Variation of Animals and Plants Under Domestication*, which showed how rapidly some organisms had evolved under artificial selection, the selective breeding of plants and animals by humans. *The Descent of Man, and Selection in Relation to Sex*, published in 1871, discussed human evolution. Later books dealt with earthworms, orchids, climbing plants, and plants that eat insects.

Darwin became very weak in 1881 and could no longer work. He died on April 19, 1882, in Downe, and was buried in Westminster Abbey among England's greatest citizens.

Darwin himself never claimed to provide proof of evolution or of the origin of species. His claim was that if evolution had occurred, a number of otherwise mysterious facts about plants and animals could be easily explained. After his death, however, direct evidence of evolution was observed, and evolution is now supported by a wealth of evidence from a variety of scientific fields.

P. A. M. DIRAC

(b. 1902–d. 1984)

O ne of the foremost theoretical physicists of the 20th century was Nobel Prize-winning English scientist P. A. M. Dirac. He was known for his work in quantum mechanics, for his theory of the spinning electron, and for having predicted the existence of antimatter.

Paul Adrien Maurice Dirac was born in Bristol, England, on August 8, 1902. His mathematical ability showed itself at an early age and was encouraged by his father, a Swiss-born teacher. Dirac studied electrical engineering at the University of Bristol. After receiving his degree he entered the University of Cambridge. In 1926, while still a graduate student, he devised a form of quantum mechanics, the laws of motion that govern particles smaller than atoms. Dirac's theoretical investigations led him to agree with other physicists that one such particle, the electron, must rotate on its axis. He also concluded that there must be states of negative energy. This idea was confirmed in 1932 when the positron—the anti-electron—was discovered. In 1933 Dirac was awarded the Nobel Prize for physics.

Dirac taught at Cambridge after receiving his doctorate there, and in 1932 he was named professor of mathematics. He served in that capacity until 1969, when he moved to the United States. In 1971 he became professor of physics at Florida State University in Tallahassee, Florida. He died in Tallahassee on October 20, 1984.

THEODOSIUS DOBZHANSKY

(b. 1900–d. 1975)

A Russian American scientist, Theodosius Dobzhansky had a major influence on 20th-century thought and research in genetics and the study of evolution. From 1918 he published more than 400 research papers that provide important factual evidence for modern evolutionary theory.

Theodosius Dobzhansky was born on January 25, 1900, in Nemirov, Russia. He began school at age 10 and graduated from the University of Kiev in 1921. In 1927 he went to Columbia University in New York City to study genetics. He taught for several years in California then returned to Columbia, where he spent most of his teaching career. He became a United States citizen in 1937.

Dobzhansky's work was involved with that of other theorists who were trying to link Charles Darwin's theory of evolution with Gregor Mendel's theory of genetics. Dobzhansky's book *Genetics and the Origin of Species*, published in 1937, was the first substantial synthesis of these related subjects. Dobzhansky's most important experiments showed that genes could vary far more than geneticists had previously believed.

35

After retiring, he moved in 1971 to the University of California at Davis. He died in Davis, California, on December 18, 1975.

GERALD MAURICE EDELMAN

(b. 1929–d. 2014)

American physician and physical chemist Gerald Maurice Edelman explored the structure of antibodies—proteins that are produced by the body in response to infection. For that work, he shared the Nobel Prize for physiology or medicine in 1972 with British biochemist Rodney Porter. Edelman also made significant contributions to developmental biology and neurobiology.

Gerald Maurice Edelman was born on July 1, 1929, in Queens, New York. He received an M.D. degree from the University of Pennsylvania, in Philadelphia, Pennaylvania, (1954) and then served two years in the United States Army Medical Corps in Paris. During that time he became intrigued by questions concerning the immune system, and upon his return to the United States he enrolled at Rockefeller Institute (now called Rockefeller University) in New York City. He earned a Ph.D. in physical chemistry in 1960 and continued his immunological research as a member of the faculty at Rockefeller, becoming a full professor in 1966.

As a graduate student, Edelman began to study antibodies, and by 1969 he and his colleagues had constructed a precise model of an antibody molecule. Edelman's group narrowly beat a rival group of British investigators led by Porter to this goal. Both researchers were awarded the Nobel Prize for the enormous contributions they made to the field of immunology.

In the 1970s Edelman shifted his research to focus on questions outside of immunology: specifically, how the body—the brain in particular—develops. In 1975 he discovered substances called cell adhesion molecules (CAMs), which "glue" cells together to form tissues. Edelman found that, as the brain develops, CAMs bind neurons together to form the brain's basic circuitry. His work led to the construction of a general theory of brain development and function called neuronal group selection, which he explained in a trilogy of books (1987–89) for a scientific audience and in *Bright Air, Brilliant Fire: On the Matter of the Mind* (1992) for laypersons. He also wrote *Wider than the Sky: The Phenomenal Gift of Consciousness* (2004) and *Second Nature: Brain Science and Human Knowledge* (2006).

From 1981 Edelman served as director of the Neurosciences Institute, which he founded at Rockefeller University. In 1993 he moved the institute to the La Jolla neighborhood of San Diego. From 1995 the institute was part of the Scripps Research Institute campus; it moved to another location in La Jolla in 2012. Edelman also formed and chaired (1992) the neurobiology department of the Scripps Research Institute and was a member (from 1996) of the Skaggs Institute for Chemical Biology at Scripps.

ALBERT EINSTEIN

(b. 1879–d. 1955)

Any list of the greatest thinkers in history will contain the name of the brilliant physicist Albert Einstein. His theories of relativity led to entirely new ways of thinking about time, space, matter, energy, and gravity. Einstein's work led to such scientific advances as the control of atomic energy and to some of the investigations of space currently being made by astrophysicists.

Einstein was born in Ulm, Germany, on March 14, 1879, of Jewish parents. He was a shy and curious child. He attended a rigorous Munich elementary school where he showed an interest in science and mathematics but did poorly in other areas of study. He finished high school and technical college in Switzerland. At age 22 he became a Swiss citizen. In 1903 he married Mileva Mareć. They had two sons but were later divorced. He married his widowed cousin Elsa in 1919.

In 1902 Einstein became an examiner in the Swiss patent office

Albert Einstein.

at Bern. In 1905, at age 26, he published five major research papers in an important German physics journal. He received a doctorate for the first paper. Publication of the next four papers forever changed mankind's view of the universe. The first one provided a theory explaining Brownian movement, the zigzag motion of microscopic particles in suspension. Einstein suggested that the movement was caused by the random motion of molecules of the suspension medium as they bounced against the suspended particles.

A second paper laid the foundation for the photon, or quantum, theory of light. In it he proposed that light is composed of separate packets of energy, called quanta or photons, that have some of the properties of particles and some of the properties of waves. The paper redefined the theory of light. It also explained the photoelectric effect, the emission of electrons from some solids when they are struck by light. Television and other inventions are practical applications of Einstein's discoveries.

A third paper, which had its beginnings in an essay he wrote at age 16, contained the "special theory of relativity." Einstein showed that time and motion are relative to the observer if the speed of light is constant and natural laws are the same everywhere in the universe. This paper introduced an entirely new concept.

The fourth paper was a mathematical addition to the special

theory of relativity. Here Einstein presented his famous formula, $E = mc^2$, known as the energy-mass relation. What it says is that the energy (E) inherent in a mass (m) equals the mass multiplied by the velocity of light squared (c^2). The formula shows that a small particle of matter is the equivalent of an enormous quantity of energy. These papers established Einstein's status as being among the most respected physicists in Europe.

In 1916 Einstein published his general theory of relativity. In it he proposed that gravity is not a force, a previously accepted theory, but a curved field in the space-time continuum that is created by the presence of mass.

Between 1909 and 1914 Einstein taught theoretical physics in Switzerland and Germany. Worldwide fame came to him in 1919 when the Royal Society of London announced that predictions made in his general theory of relativity had been confirmed. He was awarded the Nobel Prize for physics two years later; however, the prize was for his work in theoretical physics, not relativity theories, which were still considered to be controversial.

Einstein spoke out frequently against nationalism, the exalting of one nation above all others. He opposed war and violence and supported Zionism, the movement to establish a Jewish homeland in Palestine. When the Nazis came to power in Germany in 1933, they denounced his ideas, seized his property, and burned his books. That year he moved to the United States. In 1940 he became an American citizen.

Beginning in the 1920s Einstein tried to establish a mathematical relationship between electromagnetism and gravitation. He spent the rest of his life on this unsuccessful attempt to explain all of the properties of matter and energy in a single mathematical formula.

In 1939, shortly before the outbreak of World War II in Europe, Einstein learned that two German chemists had split the uranium atom. Enrico Fermi, an Italian physicist who lived in the United States, proposed that a chain-reaction splitting of uranium atoms could release enormous quantities of energy. That same year Einstein wrote to President Franklin D. Roosevelt warning him that this scientific knowledge could lead to Germany's development of an atomic bomb. He suggested that the United States begin preparations for its own atomic bomb research. Einstein's urging led to the creation of the Manhattan Project and the development of the first two atomic bombs in 1945. Einstein died in Princeton, New Jersey, on April 18, 1955.

MICHAEL FARADAY

(b. 1791–d. 1867)

The English physicist and chemist Michael Faraday made many notable contributions to chemistry and electricity. When the great scientist Sir Humphry Davy was asked what he considered his greatest discovery, he answered, "Michael Faraday."

Faraday was born in Newington, Surrey, England, on September 22, 1791. The son of a blacksmith, he was apprenticed to a bookbinder at age 14 and read all the scientific books in the shop. Young Faraday attended lectures by Sir Humphry Davy. He made careful notes and sent them to Davy, asking for a job. Impressed by the boy's zeal, the scientist took Faraday into his laboratory as an assistant.

Acting on hints from Davy, he succeeded in liquefying gas by compression. When he discovered the hydrocarbon benzene in 1825, he became the father of an entire branch of organic chemistry. His laws of electrolysis, formulated in 1833, linked chemistry and electricity.

Faraday's greatest achievement was the discovery of electromagnetic induction. He found in 1831 that when he moved a magnet through a coil of wire, a current was produced. From this discovery the electric generator—the heart of all modern electric power plants—was developed.

Late in his career Faraday discovered the rotation of the plane of polarization of light in a strong magnetic field. His work in electromagnetism led James Clerk Maxwell to the theory that linked electricity, magnetism, and light. An indirect result of both Faraday's and Maxwell's work was the invention of radio. Faraday died at Hampton Court, Surrey, on August 25, 1867.

Michael Faraday.

ENRICO FERMI

(b. 1901–d. 1954)

On December 2, 1942, the first man-made and self-sustaining nuclear chain reaction was achieved, resulting in the controlled release of nuclear energy. This feat took place in a squash court beneath the stands of an unused football stadium at the University of Chicago. The scientist who led the achievement was Enrico Fermi. The first practical use of the ability to control nuclear energy was in the atom bombs that were used at the end of World War II.

Enrico Fermi was born on September 29, 1901, in Rome, Italy. He was the youngest of three children. His father was a railroad worker, and his mother a schoolteacher. At 17 Fermi entered the University of Pisa on a scholarship. He was soon teaching theoretical physics to his own physics instructor.

In 1922 he earned his doctorate in the subject, and after further study in Göttingen, Germany, and in Leiden, Netherlands, he began teaching at the University of Rome. There Fermi met Laura Capon, a science student at the university who became his wife in 1928. They had a daughter and a son. In 1934 Fermi worked out a theory of beta-ray disintegration in radioactivity. Soon he was experimenting with neutrons and learned to make about 40 chemical elements radioactive. For this work he won the Nobel Prize in physics in 1938.

To escape fascism in Italy, the Fermi family immigrated to the United States after going to Sweden to accept the Nobel Prize. Fermi taught at Columbia University in New York City and did research on uranium. He became a United States citizen in 1944.

On December 7, 1941, the United States entered World War II. Early in 1942 Fermi transferred to the University of Chicago. In a squash court under the football stadium he developed a method of causing nuclear fission. With this method he and his group produced a chain reaction that released the explosive nuclear energy.

After the war Fermi continued as a University of Chicago professor.

In 1954, he was given the first special Atomic Energy Commission award of 25,000 dollars. Several days later, on November 28, he died of cancer in Chicago.

RICHARD P. FEYNMAN

(b. 1918–d. 1988)

The influential U.S. physicist Richard Feynman was corecipient of the 1965 Nobel Prize in physics for work in correcting inaccuracies in earlier quantum-electrodynamics formulations. He introduced simple diagrams—now called Feynman diagrams—to depict complicated mathematical expressions needed to describe systems of interacting particles. His work, which tied together all the varied phenomena at work in light, radio, electricity, and magnetism, altered the way scientists understand the nature of waves and particles. Famed for his wit, he also wrote best-selling books on science.

Richard Phillips Feynman was born in New York, New York, on May 11, 1918. He received his Ph.D. from Princeton University.

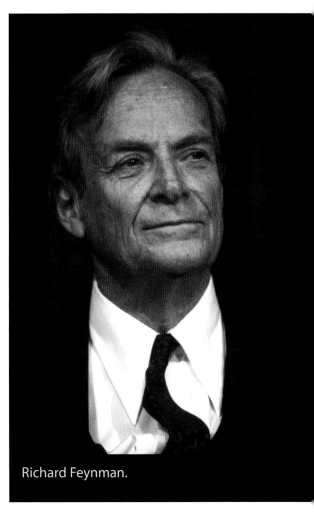

Richard Feynman.

During World War II he worked on the Manhattan Project, which produced the first atomic bombs. In 1950 Feynman became a professor at the California Institute of Technology, where he remained for the rest of his career. He died on February 15, 1988, in Los Angeles, California.

ANDREW Z. FIRE

(b. 1959–)

Andrew Z. Fire was a corecipient, with Craig C. Mello, of the Nobel Prize for physiology or medicine in 2006 for discovering a mechanism for controlling the flow of genetic information. Fire was born on April 27, 1959, in Stanford, California. He received a bachelor's degree in mathematics (1978) from the University of California, Berkeley. He was subsequently accepted into the graduate biology program at the Massachusetts Institute of Technology (MIT), where he worked with American molecular biologist Philip A. Sharp, who was awarded the 1993 Nobel Prize for physiology or medicine for his independent discovery of introns—long sections of DNA that do not encode proteins but are located within genes. Fire received a Ph.D. in biology from MIT in 1983 and then went to Cambridge, England, joining the Medical Research Council (MRC) Laboratory of Molecular Biology. At Cambridge, Fire worked with South African-born biologist Sydney Brenner and studied the genetic mechanisms that influence the early development of the nematode *Caenorhabditis elegans.*

In 1986 Fire joined the staff at the Carnegie Institution in Baltimore, Maryland, where he conducted his prizewinning research. Working with Mello, Fire helped discover RNA interference (RNAi), a mechanism in which genes are silenced by double-stranded RNA. Naturally occurring in plants, animals, and humans, RNAi regulates gene activity and helps defend against viral infection. The two men published their findings in 1998. Possible applications of RNAi include developing treatments for such diseases as AIDS, cancer, and hepatitis.

In 2003 Fire joined the faculty at Stanford University, taking professorships in pathology and genetics. His later research was concerned with understanding the mechanisms that enable cells to distinguish foreign DNA and RNA from the cells' own genetic material. This work was aimed in part at elucidating the role of RNAi in silencing the activity of foreign genetic material introduced into cells by infectious agents. Fire also investigated the role of RNAi and other genetic mechanisms in enabling cells to adapt to changes that occur throughout an organism's development.

In addition to the Nobel Prize, Fire received several other major awards during his career, including the Meyenburg Prize (2002) from the German Cancer Research Center, the Wiley Prize (2003), and the National Academy of Sciences Award in Molecular Biology (2003).

ALEXANDER FLEMING

(b. 1881–d. 1955)

Penicillin was discovered in September 1928. It has saved millions of lives by stopping the growth of the bacteria that are responsible for blood poisoning and many other once fatal diseases. This miracle drug was discovered and given to the world by Alexander Fleming, a physician and research bacteriologist at St. Mary's Hospital Medical School in London.

Alexander Fleming was born on August 6, 1881, at Lochfield, Ayrshire, Scotland. He grew up on a farm. For two years he attended Kilmarnock Academy. When he was 13 years old he went to London to live with an older brother. He worked for five years as a clerk in a shipping company. When he was 20 he won a scholarship to St. Mary's Hospital Medical School. Fleming won practically every academic honor and on his graduation was offered a position as research bacteriologist with the hospital. He was associated with St. Mary's for the rest of his life. In the last years of his life he was director of its Wright-Fleming Institute of Microbiology.

In World War I Fleming served as a medical captain, specializing in the study and treatment of wounds. He was deeply impressed by the high death rate from bacterial infection of wounds. His discovery of penicillin greatly reduced the death rate from wounds in World War II.

Fleming was studying deadly bacteria in 1928 when he made his dramatic discovery. Always retiring and modest, he attributed it to "the

45

greatest fortune." However, it was fortune combined with a gift for scientific observation and a genius for research.

For examination purposes Fleming had removed the cover of the bacteria culture plate with which he was working. A mold formed on the exposed culture. A less gifted scientist would have thrown away the accidentally contaminated culture. Fleming, however, noticed that in the area surrounding the mold, the bacteria had disappeared.

He kept a strain of the mold alive and began testing it on laboratory animals. In 1929 he published his first medical paper proving that a lowly mold from soil was a powerful microbe killer that did not injure human tissue.

For years chemists were unable to extract enough pure concentrated penicillin to use in medicine. Fleming kept his mold, but the world of science almost forgot it. Then in 1938 a team of Oxford University scientists, headed by Howard Florey and Ernst B. Chain, remembered the research paper of nine years earlier. World War II interfered with the large-scale manufacture of penicillin in Great Britain. But methods for its mass production, purification, and stabilization were developed in the United States, in cooperation with the Department of Agriculture. Fleming was knighted in 1944 in recognition of his work. He also discovered lysozyme, an antibacterial agent in tears and saliva. In 1945 he shared the Nobel Prize for physiology or medicine with Florey and Chain.

He married Sarah McElroy in 1915. They had one son, Robert, who was born in 1924. Fleming's first wife died in 1949. In 1953 he married a Greek research bacteriologist, Amalia Coutsouris. Fleming died in London on March 11, 1955.

ROSALIND FRANKLIN

(b. 1920–d. 1958)

A British biophysicist, Rosalind Franklin is best known for her contributions to the discovery of the molecular structure of deoxyribonucleic acid (DNA). DNA is the chief substance composing chromosomes and genes, the hereditary material. When Francis Crick, James Watson, and Maurice Wilkins were awarded the 1962 Nobel Prize for physiology

Rosalind Franklin.

or medicine for determining the structure of the DNA molecule, many scientists believed that Franklin should have been honored with them.

Born in London on July 25, 1920, Rosalind Elsie Franklin won a scholarship to Newnham College, Cambridge. After graduation in 1941 she began research on the physical structure of coals and carbonized coals. Working in Paris from 1947 to 1950, she gained skill in using X-ray diffraction as an analytical technique. (X-ray diffraction is a method of analyzing the crystal structure of materials by passing X-rays through them and observing the diffraction, or scattering, image of the rays.) Franklin used this technique to describe the structure of carbons with more precision than had previously been possible. She also determined that there are two distinct classes of carbons—those that form graphite when they are heated to high temperatures and those that do not.

In 1951 Franklin joined the King's College Medical Research Council biophysics unit. With Raymond Gosling she conducted X-ray diffraction studies of the molecular structure of DNA. Based on these studies, she at first concluded that the structure was helical (having spiral arms). Later research caused her to change her mind, and it was left to Watson and Crick to develop the double-helix model of the molecule that proved to be consistent with DNA's known properties. Some of the data used by those scientists in their successful effort, however, was first produced by Franklin.

From 1953 until her death on April 16, 1958, Franklin worked at the crystallography laboratory of Birkbeck College, London. There she published her earlier work on coals and helped determine the structure of the tobacco mosaic virus.

GALEN OF PERGAMUM

(b. 129–d. 199?)

The most significant physician of the ancient world after Hippocrates, Galen achieved great fame throughout the Roman Empire. He was a physician and philosopher and the founder of experimental physiology. His many writings influenced the development of medicine for 1,400 years and were partly responsible for the emergence of science in Europe during the Renaissance.

Galen was born in 129 in Pergamum (now Bergama) in Asia Minor. In that city was the chief shrine of Aesculapius, the god of healing. Attached to the shrine was a school of medicine, where the young Galen met many of the famous teachers and philosophers of his time. There was also a troupe of gladiators maintained by the school's director. These provided Galen and other students of medicine the chance to study wounds and the effects of medical treatment. Galen continued his studies in Smyrna and for a time wandered about the Middle East, taking time to visit the great medical school at Alexandria in Egypt. In 157 he returned home and became chief physician to the gladiators.

In 161 Galen traveled to Rome, where he soon earned a reputation as an outstanding healer. In about 168 the Emperor Marcus Aurelius appointed Galen physician to his son Commodus, who later became emperor. This afforded Galen the opportunity to study and to write. His more than 400 treatises were on many subjects, including philosophy and drama. His many medical writings showed penetrating and often accurate observations on the human anatomy, including heart, liver, kidney, bladder, and nerve functions. Late in the Middle Ages many of his texts were translated by Muslim Arab scholars and eventually found their way into Latin versions. Galen died in about 199, probably in Rome.

GALILEO

(b. 1564–d. 1642)

Modern physics owes its beginning to Galileo, who was the first astronomer to use a telescope. By discovering four satellites of the planet Jupiter, he gave visual evidence that supported the Copernican theory. Galileo thus helped disprove much of the medieval thinking in science.

Galileo Galilei, who is generally known only by his first name, was born in Pisa, Italy, on February 15, 1564. His family belonged to the nobility but was not rich. His father sent him to study medicine at the local university. Galileo, however, soon turned to a career in science.

In 1583 Galileo discovered the law of the pendulum by watching a chandelier swing in the cathedral at Pisa. He timed it with his pulse and found that, whether it swung in a wide or a narrow arc, it always took the same time to complete an oscillation. He thus gave society the first reliable means of keeping time.

A lecture on geometry kindled his interest in mathematics, and he got his father's consent to change his studies. Lack of money forced him to leave school in 1585, and he became a lecturer at the Academy of Florence. The next year he attracted attention with discoveries in hydrostatics. His work in dynamics won him an appointment as lecturer on mathematics at the University of Pisa in 1589.

He soon made enemies with his arguments against what he considered mistakes in the science of the day. According to a popular story, he dropped weights from the Leaning Tower of Pisa to prove his views concerning falling bodies. His writings, however, do not mention such an experiment. In any case, resentment against his views drove him out of Pisa in 1591.

In 1592 the University of Padua offered Galileo a professorship in mathematics. About 1609, after word from Holland of Hans Lippershey's newly invented telescope reached him, he built his own version of the instrument. He developed magnifying power until on January 7, 1610, he saw four satellites of Jupiter. He also saw the mountains and craters on the Moon and found the Milky Way to be a dense collection of stars.

Galileo moved to Florence in September 1610 and was a philosopher and mathematician there for many years. In 1609 Johannes Kepler published his laws of planetary motion based upon the Copernican theory. Galileo supported this view strongly. In 1616 he received a formal warning that the theory was contrary to the teachings of the Roman Catholic Church. Nevertheless, he again supported the Copernican view in a dialogue, *The Great Systems of the Universe*.

During his last eight years Galileo lived near Florence under house arrest for having "held and taught" Copernican doctrine. He became blind in 1637 but continued to work until his death on January 8, 1642. Nearly 342 years later, Galileo was pardoned by Pope John Paul II, and the church finally accepted his teachings.

Galileo.

Galileo's contributions to mechanics include the law of falling bodies, the fact that the path of a projectile is a parabola, the demonstration of the laws of equilibrium, and the principle of flotation. He devised a simple thermometer and inspired a pupil, Evangelista Torricelli, to invent the barometer. Galileo's great contribution to scientific thinking was the principle of inertia. Before his time everyone followed Aristotle's theory that when an object moved, something had to act continuously to keep it moving. Galileo countered this with the theory that if a body is moving freely, something must happen to stop it or to make it change direction.

GEORGE GAMOW

(b. 1904–d. 1968)

The Russian-born American nuclear physicist and cosmologist George Gamow was one of the foremost advocates of the bigbang theory, according to which the universe was formed in a colossal explosion that took place billions of years ago. In addition, his work on deoxyribonucleic acid (DNA) made a basic contribution to modern genetic theory.

Gamow was born Georgy Antonovich Gamov on March 4, 1904, in Odessa (at the time part of the Russian Empire, but now in Ukraine). He attended Leningrad (now St. Petersburg) University, where he studied briefly with A. A. Friedmann, a mathematician and cosmologist who suggested that the universe should be expanding. At that time Gamow did not pursue Friedmann's suggestion, preferring instead to delve into quantum theory. After graduating in 1928, he traveled to Göttingen, where he developed his quantum theory of radioactivity, the first successful explanation of the behavior of radioactive elements, some of which decay in seconds while others decay over thousands of years.

His achievement earned him a fellowship at the Copenhagen Institute of Theoretical Physics (1928–29), where he continued his investigations in theoretical nuclear physics. There he proposed his "liquid drop" model of atomic nuclei, which served as the basis for the modern theories of nuclear fission and fusion. He also collaborated with F.

Houtermans and R. Atkinson in developing a theory of the rates of ther-monuclear reactions inside stars.

In 1934, after emigrating from the Soviet Union, Gamow was named professor of physics at George Washington University in Washington, D.C. There he collaborated with Edward Teller in developing a theory of beta decay (1936), a nuclear decay process in which an electron is emitted.

Soon after, Gamow resumed his study of the relations between small-scale nuclear processes and cosmology. He used his knowledge of nuclear reactions to interpret stellar evolution, collaborating with Teller on a theory of the internal structures of red giant stars (1942). From his work on stellar evolution, Gamow postulated that the Sun's energy results from thermonuclear processes.

Gamow and Teller were proponents of the expanding-universe the-ory that had been advanced by Friedmann, Edwin Hubble, and Georges LeMaître. Gamow, however, modified the theory, and he, Ralph Alpher, and Hans Bethe published this theory in a paper called "The Origin of Chemical Elements" (1948). This paper, attempting to explain the distribution of chemical elements throughout the universe, posits a pri-meval thermonuclear explosion, the big bang, that began the universe. According to the theory, after the big bang, atomic nuclei were built up by the successive capture of neutrons by the initially formed pairs and triplets.

In 1954 Gamow's scientific interests grew to encompass biochemis-try. He proposed the concept of a genetic code and maintained that the code was determined by the order of recurring triplets of nucleotides, the basic components of DNA. His proposal was vindicated during the rapid development of genetic theory that followed.

Gamow held the position of professor of physics at the University of Colorado, Boulder, from 1956 until his death. He is perhaps best known for his popular writings, designed to introduce to the non-specialist such difficult subjects as relativity and cosmology. His first such work, *Mr. Tomkins in Wonderland* (1936), gave rise to the multivol-ume "Mr. Tomkins" series (1939–67). Among his other writings are *One, Two, Three . . . Infinity* (1947), *The Creation of the Universe* (1952; revised edition, 1961), *A Planet Called Earth* (1963), and *A Star Called the Sun* (1964).

MURRAY GELL-MANN

(b. 1929–)

For his work on bringing some order to knowledge of the seemingly chaotic profusion of subatomic particles, Murray Gell-Mann was awarded the Nobel Prize for physics in 1969.

Gell-Mann was born in New York City on September 15, 1929. He entered Yale University at the age of 15 and received his bachelor's degree in physics in 1948. Three years later he obtained his doctorate at the Massachusetts Institute of Technology. After studying and doing research for a year at the Institute for Advanced Study in Princeton, New Jersey, he joined the Institute for Nuclear Studies at the University of Chicago in 1952.

Murray Gell-Mann.

In 1953 he introduced the rather whimsical concept of "strangeness" to the study of atomic particles. Strangeness was a property that accounted for previously puzzling decay patterns of certain nuclear particles. With the assignment of a strangeness quantum number and a corresponding conservation law, there arose a new interest in bringing order to the confused multiplicity of particles. Gell-Mann's efforts were assisted by the independent studies of the Japanese physicist Kazuhiko Nishijima.

In 1955 Gell-Mann joined the staff of the California Institute of Technology, where he was appointed Millikan Professor of Theoretical Physics in 1967. In 1961 he and Yuval Ne'eman, an Israeli physicist, proposed the Eightfold Way. Named after Buddha's Eightfold Path to Enlightenment, the Eightfold Way was a system for grouping all particles into a simple and orderly arrangement of families, somewhat comparable to the periodic table of elements. Because his system had gaps in it, Gell-Mann predicted, correctly, that new particles would be discovered to fit the gaps. After three years of work, the omega-minus particle was discovered in 1964, completing a major family and winning acceptance for the Eightfold Way. A further development of his studies led to Gell-Mann's theory of the existence of particles called quarks. It has been proposed that six varieties of quarks are the basic building blocks of most other particles.

JANE GOODALL

(b. 1934–)

British ethologist Jane Goodall is best known for her exceptionally detailed and long-term research on the chimpanzees of Gombe Stream National Park in Tanzania. Over the years she was able to correct a number of misunderstandings about these animals.

Goodall was born on April 3, 1934, in London, England. She was interested in animal behavior from an early age. After leaving school when she was 18 years old, she worked as a secretary and as a film production

Jane Goodall, with a chimpanzee.

assistant until she gained passage to Africa. Once there, Goodall began assisting paleontologist and anthropologist Louis Leakey. Her association with Leakey led eventually to her establishment in June 1960 of a camp in the Gombe Stream Game Reserve (now a national park) so that she could observe the behavior of chimpanzees in the region.

In 1964 Goodall married a Dutch photographer who had been sent in 1962 to Tanzania to film her work (they later divorced). The University of Cambridge awarded Goodall a Ph.D. in ethology in 1965; she was one of very few candidates to receive a doctoral degree without having first possessed a bachelor's degree. Except for short periods of absence, Goodall and her family remained in Gombe until 1975, often directing the fieldwork of other doctoral candidates. In 1977 she cofounded the Jane Goodall Institute for Wildlife Research, Education, and Conservation in California. The center later moved its headquarters to Washington, D.C.

During her research, Goodall found that chimpanzees are omnivorous, not vegetarian, and that they are capable of making and using tools.

She also discovered that they have a set of complex and highly developed social behaviors that were previously unrecognized by humans.

Goodall wrote a number of books and articles about various aspects of her work, notably *In the Shadow of Man* (1971). She summarized her years of observation in *The Chimpanzees of Gombe: Patterns of Behavior* (1986). Goodall continued to write and lecture about environmental and conservation issues into the early 21st century. The recipient of numerous honors, she was created Dame of the British Empire in 2003.

OTTO HAHN

(b. 1879–d. 1968)

The German chemist Otto Hahn is credited, along with radiochemist Fritz Strassmann, with discovering nuclear fission. This development led directly to the creation of atomic weapons during World War II and to the modern nuclear power industry. Hahn was awarded the Nobel Prize for chemistry in 1944 and shared the Enrico Fermi award in 1966 with Strassmann and Austrian physicist Lise Meitner.

Hahn was born on March 8, 1879, in Frankfurt am Main, Germany. He attended the universities of Marburg and Munich and received his doctorate from Marburg in 1901. After a year of military service and two years teaching at Marburg, he studied radioactivity in London and Montreal. He returned to Germany to work in the chemistry laboratory of the University of Berlin. From 1912 until 1944 he was at the Kaiser Wilhelm Institute for Chemistry (later the Max Planck Society for the Advancement of Science).

During World War I Hahn was a chemical-warfare expert. After the war he and Meitner announced the discovery of the radioactive element protactinium. Inspired by Enrico Fermi's work on bombarding uranium with subatomic particles, Hahn and his associates obtained results indicating that atoms were split in the process. To this action they gave the name nuclear fission. The implications of this discovery were immediately apparent to scientists. After time in England after World War II, Hahn returned to Germany. He died at Göttingen on July 28, 1968.

EDMOND HALLEY

(b. 1656–d. 1742)

The English astronomer and mathematician Edmond Halley was the first to calculate the orbit of a comet later named after him. He also encouraged Sir Isaac Newton to write his *Philosophiae Naturalis Principia Mathematica*, which Halley published in 1687 at his own expense.

Halley was born in Haggerston, Shoreditch, near London, on November 8, 1656. He began his education at St. Paul's School, London, and in 1673 entered Queen's College at Oxford University. There he learned of John Flamsteed's project at the Royal Greenwich Observatory using the telescope to compile an accurate catalog of stars visible in the Northern Hemisphere. Halley proposed to do the same thing for the Southern Hemisphere. Leaving Oxford without his degree, he sailed for the island of St. Helena in the South Atlantic in 1676. His results were published in a star catalog in 1678, establishing the youth as a prominent astronomer. Halley, who sometimes spelled his first name Edmund, published the first meteorological chart in 1686 and the first magnetic charts of the Atlantic and Pacific areas, which were used in navigation for many years after his death. Continuing his work in observational astronomy, he published in 1705 *A Synopsis of the Astronomy of Comets*, in which he described 24 comets.

He accurately predicted the return in 1758 of a comet—now known as Halley's comet—previously observed in 1531, 1607, and 1682. Halley died in Greenwich, England, on January 14, 1742.

WILLIAM HARVEY

(b. 1578–d. 1657)

From dissecting many creatures, including humans, English physician William Harvey discovered the nature of blood circulation and the function of the heart as a pump. Before his discoveries blood was thought to ebb and flow through the body by the contraction of arteries. Harvey's work also laid down the foundations of physiology, the study of body functions.

William Harvey was born on April 1, 1578, in Folkestone, Kent, England. He was the oldest of the seven sons of Thomas Harvey. At age 10 he was sent to the King's School in Canterbury, and at 16 he entered Gonville and Caius College, Cambridge, where he received a bachelor's degree in 1597.

Harvey then studied medicine at the University of Padua in Italy, the finest medical school of its time. One of his teachers was Hieronymus Fabricius, a noted surgeon and anatomist who had already discovered the one-way valves in veins, but was not sure of their purpose. Harvey later proved that they prevent blood from flowing backward. He returned to London after receiving his medical degree in 1602.

Shortly after his return to England Harvey married Elizabeth Browne, daughter of a physician to Queen Elizabeth I. In 1607 he received a fellowship at the Royal College of Physicians, and in 1609 he became assistant physician. He was then a physician at St. Bartholomew's Hospital until 1643.

In 1618 Harvey was appointed one of the physicians to King James I. When King Charles I ascended to the throne Harvey became his personal physician. King Charles took a personal interest in Harvey's research in circulation and growth, and he provided Harvey with animals for experimentation.

From 1615 to 1656 Harvey was appointed to a college lectureship. The manuscript of the notes on which the lectures were based is entitled *Lectures on the Whole of Anatomy*. His famous book *On the Motion of the Heart and Blood in Animals*, published in 1628, gave a unique and accurate account of the circulatory system. The book made Harvey famous throughout Europe despite initial attacks on it.

Harvey explained that blood does not contain bubbles of air. He proved that blood does not pass through the heart's septum, and he explained the function of the valves in the heart and larger veins. Harvey died in London on June 3, 1657.

STEPHEN HAWKING

(b. 1942–)

O ne of the most admired and brilliant theoretical physicists of the late 20th and early 21st centuries, Stephen Hawking became a widely known celebrity as well after his book *A Brief History of Time: From the Big Bang to Black Holes* unexpectedly became a best-seller in 1988 (a motion picture based on the book followed). He specialized in the study of black holes, the elusive remains of collapsed giant stars. He also worked in the areas of general relativity, thermodynamics, and quantum mechanics in seeking to understand how the universe began. His achievements have proved all the more amazing because he suffered since the early 1960s from the severely debilitating amyotrophic lateral sclerosis (Lou Gehrig's disease), which gradually destroys the nerve and muscle systems.

Stephen Hawking.

Stephen William Hawking was born on January 8, 1942, in Oxford, England, and grew up in London. He attended St. Albans School and entered Oxford University in 1959. Upon graduating in 1962 he moved to Cambridge University to study theoretical astronomy and cosmology. It was at this time he was diagnosed with amyotrophic lateral sclerosis. As the disease worsened, Hawking was confined to a motorized wheelchair. In time, he was unable to write and barely able to speak. He, however, proceeded to work on his doctorate and in 1965 married a fellow student, Jane Wilde. (The marriage lasted until 1990.)

After receiving his doctorate in 1966, he remained at Cambridge as a member of the department of applied mathematics. He was appointed professor of gravitational physics in 1977 and Lucasian professor of mathematics (a chair previously held by Sir Isaac Newton) in 1979. In 2008 he accepted a visiting research chair at the Perimeter Institute for Theoretical Physics in Waterloo, Ontario.

Hawking's earliest work, in collaboration with Roger Penrose, dealt with Einstein's general theory of relativity, black holes, and gravity. The great success of *A Brief History of Time* surprised him. He followed it with a series of essays, *Black Holes and Baby Universes and Other Essays*, in 1993 and with *The Universe in a Nutshell* in 2001 and *A Briefer History of Time* in 2005. Hawking received the Copley Medal from the Royal Society in 2006 and the U.S. Presidential Medal of Freedom in 2009.

WERNER HEISENBERG

(b. 1901–d. 1976)

For his work on quantum mechanics, the German physicist Werner Heisenberg received the Nobel Prize for physics in 1932. He will probably be best remembered, however, for developing the uncertainty (or indeterminacy) principle, the concept that the behavior of subatomic particles can be predicted only on the basis of probability. Isaac Newton's laws of motion, therefore, cannot be used to predict accurately the behavior of single subatomic particles.

Werner Karl Heisenberg was born on December 5, 1901, in Würzburg. He studied theoretical physics at the University of Munich and received his doctorate in 1923. From there he went to Göttingen to study under Max Born in 1924 and to Copenhagen, Denmark, to work with Niels Bohr. His original quantum theory was published in 1925–26 and his uncertainty principle in 1927. With Bohr he developed the principle of complementarity, a concept of measurement in physics that many physicists, including Albert Einstein, refused to accept.

From 1927 until 1941 Heisenberg was professor of theoretical physics at the University of Leipzig. During World War II he worked with Otto Hahn at the Kaiser Wilhelm Institute for Physics in Berlin on developing a nuclear reactor. Secretly hostile to the Nazi regime, Heisenberg worked to keep Germany from developing effective nuclear weapons. After the war he became director of the Max Planck Institute for Physics. He died in Munich on February 1, 1976.

HERMANN VON HELMHOLTZ

(b. 1821–d. 1894)

The law of the conservation of energy was developed by Hermann von Helmholtz. This creative and versatile scientist made fundamental contributions to physiology, optics, electrodynamics, mathematics, and meteorology. He believed that all science could be reduced to the laws of classical mechanics, which encompassed matter, force, and energy as the whole of reality.

Hermann Ludwig Ferdinand Helmholtz was born in Prussia (now part of Germany) in Potsdam, on August 31, 1821. His first schooling was at home, where his parents taught him Latin, Greek, French, and other languages as well as the philosophy of Immanuel Kant. After graduating from the local gymnasium, or secondary school, he entered the Friedrich Wilhelm Medical Institute in Berlin in 1838. After graduation in 1843 he served as an army doctor for five years.

In 1848 he was appointed assistant at the Anatomical Museum and professor at the Academy of Fine Arts in Berlin. For the rest of his career he did research and taught successively at the Physiological Institute in Königsberg, the University of Bonn, Heidelberg University, and the University of Berlin. He was elevated to the German nobility in 1882. In 1888 he became the first director of the Physico-Technical Institute in Berlin and remained in that post the rest of his life. He died in Berlin on September 8, 1894.

Helmholtz's two most significant publications were *On the Sensation of Tone as a Physiological Basis for the Theory of Music* (1863) and *Handbook of Physiological Optics* (1867). His paper "On the Conservation of Force" was issued in 1847. In all his work, ranging from physiology to electrodynamics, he relied on classical mechanics for his reasoning. A decade after his death Albert Einstein would begin publishing the papers that permanently undermined the theories held by Helmholtz.

WILLIAM HERSCHEL

(b. 1738–d. 1822)

The founder of modern stellar astronomy was a German-born organist, William Herschel. His discovery of Uranus in 1781 was the first identification of a planet since ancient times. Herschel developed theories of the structure of nebulae and the evolution of stars, cataloged many binary stars, and made significant modifications in the reflecting telescope. He also proved that the solar system moves through space and discovered infrared radiation.

Friedrich Wilhelm Herschel was born in Hannover, Germany, on November 15, 1738. When he was 21 he moved to England to work as a musician. He later taught music, wrote symphonies, and conducted. Although he did not become a professional astronomer until he was 43 years old, he worked night after night to develop a "natural history" of the heavens. Whenever the Moon and weather permitted, he observed the sky in the company of his sister, Caroline, who recorded his observations. On overcast nights, William would post a watchman to summon him if the clouds should break. In the daytime, Caroline would summarize the results of their work while he directed the construction of telescopes, many of which he sold to supplement their income. His largest instrument, too cumbersome for regular use, had a mirror made of speculum metal, with a diameter of 48 inches (122 cm) and a focal length of 40 feet (12 m). Completed in 1789, it became one of the technical wonders of the 18th century.

Herschel discovered Uranus with the first reflecting telescope that he built. The discovery brought him an appointment as astronomer for George III, and he was able to spend all his time studying the stars. Herschel's observations of binary stars demonstrated that gravity governed the stars as well as the solar system. He died in Slough, England, on August 25, 1822.

Caroline Herschel executed many of the calculations connected with her brother's studies and, on her own, detected by telescope three nebulae in 1783 and eight comets from 1786 to 1797. William Herschel's son, John Herschel, continued his father's study of binary stars and made the first telescopic study of the Southern Hemisphere while at the Cape of Good Hope, South Africa (1834–38). A chemist and physicist, he also made contributions to photography, spectroscopic analysis, and crystallography.

PETER HIGGS

(b. 1929–)

British physicist Peter Higgs was awarded the 2013 Nobel Prize for physics for proposing the existence of the Higgs boson, a subatomic particle that is the carrier particle of a field that endows all elementary particles with mass through its interactions with them. He shared the prize with Belgian physicist François Englert.

Peter Ware Higgs was born on May 29, 1929, Newcastle upon Tyne, Northumberland, England. He received a bachelor's degree (1950), master's degree (1951), and doctorate (1954) in physics from King's College, University of London. He was a research fellow (1955–56) at the University of Edinburgh and then a research fellow (1956–58) and lecturer (1959–60) at the University of London. He became a lecturer in mathematical physics at Edinburgh in 1960 and spent the remainder of his career there, becoming a reader in mathematical physics (1970–80) and a professor of theoretical physics (1980–96). He retired in 1996.

Higgs's earliest work was in molecular physics and concerned calculating the vibrational spectra of molecules. In 1956 he began working in quantum field theory. He wrote two papers in 1964 describing what later became known as the Higgs mechanism, in which a scalar field (that is, a field present at all points in space) gives particles mass. To Higgs's surprise, the journal to which he submitted the second paper rejected it. When Higgs revised the paper, he made the significant addition that his theory predicted the existence of a heavy boson. (The Higgs mechanism was independently discovered in 1964 by Englert and Belgian physicist Robert Brout and by another group consisting of American physicists Gerald Guralnik and Carl Hagen and British physicist Tom Kibble. However, neither group mentioned the possibility of a massive boson.)

In the late 1960s American physicist Steven Weinberg and Pakistani physicist Abdus Salam independently incorporated Higgs's ideas into what later became known as electroweak theory to describe the origin of particle masses. After the discovery of the W and Z particles in 1983, the only remaining part of electroweak theory that needed confirmation was the Higgs field and its boson. Particle physicists searched for the particle for decades, and in July 2012 scientists at the Large Hadron Collider at CERN announced, with Higgs in attendance, that they had detected an interesting signal that was likely from a Higgs boson with a mass of 125–126 gigaelectron volts (billion electron volts; GeV). Definitive confirmation that the particle was the Higgs boson was announced in March 2013.

Higgs became a fellow of the Royal Society in 1983. He received many honors for his work, including the Wolf Prize in physics (2004, shared with Brout and Englert) and the J. J. Sakurai Prize (2010, shared with Brout, Englert, Guralnik, Hagen, and Kibble).

HIPPOCRATES

(b. 460?–d. 377? BCE)

The first name in the history of medicine is Hippocrates, a physician from the island of Cos in ancient Greece. Known as the Father of Medicine, Hippocrates has long been associated with the Hippocratic

Oath, a document he did not write but which sets forth the obligations, ideals, and ethics of physicians. In a modified form the oath is still often required of medical students upon graduation.

Very little is known of the life of Hippocrates. He was a contemporary of the philosopher Socrates in the 5th century BCE and was mentioned by Plato in two of his dialogues. He was, in his lifetime, quite well known as a teacher and physician, and he appears to have traveled widely in Greece and Asia Minor, practicing medicine and teaching. There was presumably a medical school on Cos, in which he taught frequently. Hippocrates probably belonged to a family that had produced well-known physicians for many generations. Aristotle says in his *Politics* that Hippocrates was called "the Great Physician." Hippocrates died at Larissa in Thessaly.

A small body of writings ascribed to Hippocrates has come down to the present. How many he actually wrote will probably never be known. The number of works in ancient times was 70, but only 60 have been preserved. The earliest surviving copy dates from the 10th century CE.

The works differ greatly in their length, in the opinions expressed, and in the types of intended users. Some are for physicians, some for assistants and students, and some for laymen. A few are philosophical. It is generally agreed that the writings made up the medical library at Cos. During the 3rd or 2nd century BCE they were shipped to the great library at Alexandria, Egypt. Among the titles are *Ancient Medicine*, *Regimen in Acute Diseases*, *Wounds of the Head*, *Aphorisms*, and *Epidemics*.

ROBERT HOOKE

(b. 1635–d. 1703)

The English physicist Robert Hooke discovered the law of elasticity, known as Hooke's law, and did research in a remarkable variety of fields. Hooke was born on July 18, 1635, at Freshwater, on the Isle of Wight. In 1655 Robert Boyle employed him to construct the Boylean air pump. Five years later, Hooke discovered his law of elasticity, which states that the stretching of a solid body (e.g., metal, wood) is proportional to the force applied to it. The law laid the basis for studies of stress and strain and for understanding of elastic materials. He applied these studies in his designs for the balance springs of watches. In 1662 he was appointed curator of experiments to the Royal Society of London and was elected a fellow the following year.

One of the first men to build a Gregorian reflecting telescope, Hooke discovered the fifth star in the Trapezium, an asterism in the constellation Orion, in 1664 and first suggested that Jupiter rotates on its axis. His detailed sketches of Mars were used in the 19th century to determine that planet's rate of rotation. In 1665 he was appointed professor of geometry in Gresham College. In *Micrographia* (1665; "Small Drawings") he included his studies and illustrations of the crystal structure of snowflakes, discussed the possibility of manufacturing artificial fibers by a process similar to the spinning of the silkworm, and first used the word cell to name the microscopic honeycomb cavities in cork. His studies of microscopic fossils led him to become one of the first proponents of a theory of evolution.

He suggested that the force of gravity could be measured by utilizing the motion of a pendulum (1666) and attempted to show that Earth and the Moon follow an elliptical path around the Sun. In 1672 he discovered the phenomenon of diffraction (the bending of light rays around corners). To explain it, he offered the wave theory of light. He stated the inverse square law to describe planetary motions in 1678, a law that Newton later used in modified form. Hooke complained that he was not given sufficient credit for the law and became involved in bitter controversy with Newton. Hooke was the first man to state in general that all matter expands when heated and that air is made up of particles separated from each other by relatively large distances.

ALEXANDER VON HUMBOLDT

(b. 1769–d. 1859)

Along with Napoleon, Alexander von Humboldt was one of the most famous men of Europe during the first half of the 19th century. He was a German scholar and explorer whose interests encompassed virtually all of the natural and physical sciences. He laid the foundations for modern physical geography, geophysics, and biogeography and helped to popularize science. His interest in the Earth's geomagnetic fields led directly to the establishment of permanent observatories in British possessions around the world, one of the first instances of international scientific cooperation. Humboldt's meteorological data contributed to comparative climatology. The Humboldt Current off the west coast of South America (now called the Peru Current) was named after him.

Friedrich Wilhelm Karl Heinrich Alexander von Humboldt was born in Berlin, Germany (then Prussia), on September 14, 1769. He and his brother Wilhelm were educated at home during their early years. (Wilhelm eventually became one of Europe's most noted language scholars and educational reformers.) Alexander was at first a poor student and for some years could not decide on a career. Finally botany stirred his interest, then geology and mineralogy. He studied at the University of Göttingen and at the School of Mines in Saxony. In 1792 he obtained a position with the Prussian government's Mining Department. Humboldt worked prodigiously to improve mine safety, invented a safety lamp, and started a technical school for young miners. All the while, he was becoming convinced that his goal in life was scientific exploration.

The remainder of Humboldt's life can be divided into three segments: his expedition to South America (1799–1804); his professional life in Paris, where he organized and published the data accumulated on the expedition (1804–27); and his last years, which were spent mostly in Berlin. The Spanish government permitted him to visit Central and South America. This little-known region offered great possibilities for scientific exploration. Accompanied by the French botanist Aimé Bonpland, Humboldt covered more than 6,000 miles (9,650 kilometers) on foot, horseback, or by canoe. After the trip Humboldt went to the United States and was received by President Thomas Jefferson.

Humboldt and Bonpland returned to Europe with an immense amount of information about plants, longitude and latitude, the Earth's geomagnetism, and climate. After brief visits to Berlin and a trip to Italy

Alexander von Humboldt.

to inspect Mount Vesuvius, he settled in Paris readying the 30 volumes containing the results of the South American expedition.

Humboldt returned to Berlin at the insistence of the king of Prussia. He lectured on physical geography to large audiences and organized international scientific conferences. In 1829 he traveled through Russia into Siberia, as far as the Chinese frontier. The last 25 years were occupied chiefly with writing his *Kosmos*, one of the most ambitious scientific works ever published. In it Humboldt presented his cosmic view of the universe as a whole. He was writing the fifth volume of this work when he died in Berlin on May 6, 1859.

JAMES HUTTON

(b. 1726–d. 1797)

The Scottish scientist James Hutton originated one of the fundamental principles of geology: uniformitarianism. This principle assumes an enormously long span of time during which the different kinds of rocks composing the Earth had been formed by diverse natural processes. Although vigorously attacked at the time, this theory became the cornerstone of modern geologic studies.

Hutton was born in Edinburgh, Scotland, on June 3, 1726. He tried his hand at chemistry, law, medicine, and farming before taking up geology. With James Davie he developed a cheap process for making sal ammoniac (ammonium chloride) from coal soot, for use in industry.

With the money he made from the process he bought a farm and worked it for several years. While farming he began studying rocks and the effects of natural processes, such as rain, running water, tides, and volcanoes, on the development of the Earth. His theories received little notice until 1785 when he presented two papers on his uniformitarian principle to the Royal Society of Edinburgh. They were published in 1788, and two volumes of his *Theory of the Earth* came out in 1795. He was working on a third volume at the time of his death on March 26, 1797, in Edinburgh.

CHRISTIAAN HUYGENS

(b. 1629–d. 1695)

The shape of the rings of Saturn was discovered by Christiaan Huygens, a Dutch astronomer, mathematician, and physicist. Huygens also developed the wave theory of light and made significant contributions to the science of dynamics and the use of the pendulum in clocks. His reputation in mathematics as well as his wealth and parentage enabled him to correspond with some of the leading scientists of his time, including René Descartes, Blaise Pascal, and Gottfried Wilhelm Leibniz. Late in life he met Isaac Newton, with whose theory of gravitation he disagreed.

Huygens was born in The Hague on April 14, 1629. He was trained by his father in languages and drawing, and at 13 he began the study of

Christiaan Huygens.

71

mechanics. In 1645 he entered the University of Leiden to study mathematics and law. Two years later he transferred to the College of Breda.

At 21 he published his first treatise on mathematics and followed this with work on probability theory. At the same time, he and his older brother discovered a new method of grinding and polishing lenses for use by astronomers. In 1655 he discovered Saturn's moon Titan. He identified the components of the Orion nebula in 1656 and three years later published his discoveries of the shape of Saturn's rings. His construction of a pendulum clock with an escapement aided in his observation of planetary motion. Huygens lived in Paris from 1666 until 1681, when he returned to Holland. Written much earlier, his *Discourse on the Cause of Gravity* and *Treatise on Light* were published in 1690. He died on July 8, 1695, in The Hague.

IBN AL-HAYTHAM

(b. 965–d. 1040)

The mathematician and astronomer Ibn al-Haytham (Latinized as Alhazen, in full, Abū ʿAlī al-Ḥasan ibn al-Haytham) made significant contributions to the principles of optics and the use of scientific experiments. Ibn al-Haytham's most important work is *Kitāb al-manāẓir* (*Optics*). Although it shows some influence from Ptolemy's 2nd century CE *Optics*, it contains the correct model of vision: the passive reception by the eyes of light rays reflected from objects, not an active emanation of light rays from the eyes. It combines experiment with mathematical reasoning, even if it is generally used for validation rather than discovery. The work contains a complete formulation of the laws of reflection and a detailed investigation of refraction, including experiments involving angles of incidence and deviation. Refraction is correctly explained by light's moving slower in denser mediums. The work also contains "Alhazen's problem"— to determine the point of reflection from a plane or curved surface, given the center of the eye and the observed point—which is stated and solved by means of conic sections. Other optical works include *Ḍawʾ al-qamar*

(*On the Light of the Moon*), *al-Hāla wa-qaws quzaḥ* (*On the Halo and the Rainbow*), *Ṣūrat al-kusūf* (*On the Shape of the Eclipse*, which includes a discussion of the camera obscura), and *al-Ḍaw'* (*A Discourse on Light*).

Ibn al-Haytham's most famous astronomical work is *Hay'at al-ʿālam* (*On the Configuration of the World*), in which he presents a non-technical description of how the abstract mathematical models of Ptolemy's *Almagest* can be understood according to the natural philosophy of his time. While this early work implicitly accepts Ptolemy's models, a later work, the aptly named *al-Shukūk ʿalā Baṭlamyūs* (*Doubts about Ptolemy*), criticizes the *Almagest*, along with Ptolemy's *Planetary Hypotheses* and *Optics*.

JAMES PRESCOTT JOULE
(b.1818–d. 1889)

I t was English physicist James Prescott Joule who established that the various forms of energy—mechanical, electrical, and heat—are basically the same and can be changed, one into another. Thus he formed the basis of the law of conservation of energy, the first law of thermodynamics.

Joule studied with the noted English chemist John Dalton at the University of Manchester in 1835. Describing "Joule's law" in a paper, "On the Production of Heat by Voltaic Electricity," (1840), he stated that the heat produced in a wire by an electric current is proportional to the product of the resistance of the wire and the square of the current. In 1843 he published his value for the amount of work required to produce a unit of heat, called the mechanical equivalent of heat. He used four increasingly accurate methods of determining this value. By using different materials, he also established that heat was a form of energy regardless of the substance that was heated. In 1852 Joule and William Thomson (later Lord Kelvin) discovered that when a gas is allowed to expand without performing external work, the temperature of the gas falls. This "Joule-Thomson effect" was used to build a large refrigeration industry in the 19th century. The value of the mechanical equivalent of heat is generally represented by the letter *J*, and a standard unit of work is called the joule.

LORD KELVIN

(b. 1824–d. 1907)

William Thomson, who became Lord Kelvin of Largs (Scotland) in 1892, was one of Great Britain's foremost scientists and inventors. He published more than 650 scientific papers and patented some 70 inventions. He is known for developing a temperature scale in which −273.15°C (−459.67°F) is absolute zero. The scale is known as the absolute, or Kelvin, temperature scale. William Thomson was born on June 26, 1824, in Belfast, Ireland. The family moved to Glasgow, Scotland, in 1832, and young Thomson entered the university there when he was 10. He was a brilliant student. By the time he was 21 he had studied in Glasgow, Cambridge (England), and Paris and had published 12 scientific papers.

In 1846 he became a professor of natural philosophy at Glasgow. There he established the first physics laboratory in Great Britain. His investigations into the properties of matter made him famous.

Thomson supervised the laying of the first transatlantic cable in 1866. To improve cable communication, he also invented and put into use the mirror galvanometer for signaling and the siphon recorder for receiving. For his work he was knighted by Queen Victoria.

Sir William traveled widely in Europe and the United States, lecturing at Johns Hopkins University in Baltimore, Maryland, in 1884. He had an interest in yachting and the sea that inspired him to invent, patent, and manufacture a compass used by the British admiralty, a calculating machine that measured tides, and depth-measuring, or sounding, equipment. He coauthored the textbook *Treatise on Natural Philosophy*, which was published in 1867 and was a major influence on future physicists.

Before his death at Largs on December 17, 1907, Lord Kelvin had become an honorary member of many foreign academies and held honorary degrees from many well-known universities. He served as president of the Royal Society from 1890 to 1895.

JOHANNES KEPLER
(b. 1571–d. 1630)

The Renaissance astronomer and astrologer Johannes Kepler is best known for his discovery that the orbits in which the Earth and the other planets of the solar system travel around the Sun are elliptical, or oval, in shape. He was also the first to explain correctly how human beings see and to demonstrate what happens to light when it enters a telescope. In addition, he designed an instrument that serves as the basis of the modern refractive telescope.

Kepler was born on December 27, 1571, at Weil der Stadt in the duchy of Württemberg, now in southern Germany. He was a sickly child but had a brilliant mind. At the University of Tübingen he was greatly influenced by the theories of the astronomer Copernicus. He later taught astronomy and mathematics at the university in Graz, Austria. While there he corresponded with two other great astronomers of the time—Galileo and Tycho Brahe. In 1600 he became Tycho's assistant in Prague.

When Tycho died Kepler succeeded him as astrologer and astronomer to Rudolph II of Bohemia. His task of doing horoscopes at births and other important events in the royal family was of first importance; astronomy was secondary. Kepler, however, gave all the time he could to the outstanding astronomical problem of the day.

By Kepler's time, many astronomers had accepted that the Sun was the center of the solar system and that the Earth turned on its axis, but they still believed that the planets moved in circular orbits. Because of this, they could not explain the motions of the planets as seen from the Earth.

Kepler decided to try explaining these motions by finding another shape for the planetary orbits. Because Mars offered the most typical problem and he had Tycho's accurate observations of this planet, Kepler began with it. He tried every possible combination of circular motions in attempts to account for Mars's positions. These all failed, though once a discrepancy of only eight minutes of arc remained unaccounted for. "Out of these eight minutes," he said, "we will construct a new theory that will explain the motions of all the planets!"

After six years, hampered by poor eyesight and the clumsy mathematical methods of the day, he found the answer. Mars follows an elliptical orbit at a speed that varies according to the planet's distance from the Sun. In 1609 he published a book on the results of his work, boldly titling it *The New Astronomy*.

He then turned to the other planets and found that their motions corresponded to those of Mars. He also discovered that their periods of revolution—time required to go around the Sun—bore a precise relation to their distances from the Sun.

Kepler's great work on planetary motion is summed up in three principles, which have become known as "Kepler's laws": (1) The path of every planet in its motion about the Sun forms an ellipse, with the Sun at one focus. (2) The speed of a planet in its orbit varies so that a line joining it with the Sun sweeps over equal areas in equal times. (3) The squares of the planets' periods of revolution are proportional to the cubes of the planets' mean distances from the Sun. These laws removed all doubt that the Earth and planets go around the Sun. Later Sir Isaac Newton used Kepler's laws to establish his law of universal gravitation.

Kepler could now proceed with his task of revising the *Tabulae Rudolphinae* (*Rudolphine Tables*), an almanac of the positions of heavenly bodies that, though unsatisfactory, was the best available at the time. Kepler's new laws enabled him to predict the positions of the planets by date and hour and have proved to be substantially accurate even to the present day.

Kepler was one of the first to be informed by Galileo about his invention of the telescope, and afterward Kepler went on to do valuable pioneer work in optics. It was Kepler who invented the present-day form of astronomical telescope. His book on optics, *Dioptrics*, published in 1611, was the first of its kind and founded the scientific study of light and lenses. Kepler died on November 15, 1630, in Regensburg in Bavaria.

JEAN-BAPTISTE LAMARCK
(b. 1744–d. 1829)

The man who coined the word *biologie* ("biology") and one of the pioneers in that field was a French scientist named Lamarck. He is remembered most for his theory of evolution, that proposed that the characteristics an organism develops during its lifetime in response to its environment are inherited by, or passed on to, its offspring. Charles Darwin's theories, published 30 years after Lamarck's death, disagreed with Lamarck's conclusions, which were later discarded by most scientists as invalid.

Jean-Baptiste de Monet Lamarck was born on August 1, 1744, in Picardy. After his schooling he served in the French army from 1761 to 1768, during which time he became interested in botany and the classification of plants. In 1778 he published a three-volume work on the plants of France. After the start of the French Revolution in 1789, Lamarck promoted and became one of the originators of the Museum of Natural History, founded in Paris in 1793. He was placed in charge of the invertebrate animals at the museum, and from his work was able to revise the classification of lower animals that had been unfinished by the Swedish biologist Carolus Linnaeus. His continued study of invertebrates led to the publication of his major work, *Histoire naturelle des animaux sans vertèbres* (*The Natural History of Invertebrate Animals*, published in 1815–22). Although Lamarck's theories on evolution were discarded after Darwin, he succeeded in establishing procedures of inquiry for the study of invertebrates that were useful long after his death.

Lamarck was a generalist in science at a time when specialization was emerging. He sought the unities that underlie the natural world. This led to his increasing isolation from other scientists. He died lonely and in poverty in Paris on December 18, 1829.

PIERRE-SIMON, MARQUIS DE LAPLACE

(b. 1749–d. 1827)

One of the most brilliant astronomers in the history of the field was Pierre-Simon Laplace. This Frenchman predicted with mathematics many things that were to be seen later with powerful telescopes.

Laplace was born on March 23, 1749, in Beaumont-en-Auge, a village in Normandy. His father was poor, and Pierre-Simon received little early education. Wealthy neighbors took an interest in him, however, and sent him to the university at Caen. There he did very well in mathematics. At 18 he went to Paris with a letter explaining the principles of mechanics to give to Jean d'Alembert, a leading mathematician. D'Alembert was impressed, and he helped the young man get a position as professor of mathematics at the École Militaire.

In 1773 Laplace discovered the invariability of the planetary mean motions, establishing the solar system's stability. Another important theory supporting stability was his discovery in 1787 of the dependence of the moon's acceleration on the eccentricity of the Earth's orbit.

With the mathematician Joseph-Louis Lagrange, Laplace reviewed the studies made since Isaac Newton's time on gravitational forces in the universe. Then he wrote *Traité de mécanique céleste* (*Celestial Mechanics*), issued in five volumes from 1798 to 1827. A condensed version contained his nebular hypothesis, a theory of the origin of the solar system. Laplace won many awards for his studies and was made a marquis, but he remained modest, saying, "What we know is little. What we know not is immense." He died in Paris on March 5, 1827.

ANTOINE-LAURENT LAVOISIER

(b. 1743–d. 1794)

One of the most honored men in the history of science is the Frenchman Antoine-Laurent Lavoisier. For more than a century before his day, chemists had been hampered by a false theory about

Antoine-Laurent Lavoisier.

fire and the burning of matter. By revealing the truth about fire and burning, Lavoisier helped chemistry make its remarkable advance from that time on.

Lavoisier was born in Paris, France, on August 26, 1743, the son of a wealthy lawyer and landowner. His father bought a title of nobility and wanted an aristocratic career for the boy. Young Lavoisier preferred science, however, so his father sent him to many distinguished scholars. He eventually studied mathematics at Mazarin College under Abbé Lecaille and botany under the renowned botanist Bernard de Jussieu. Lavoisier was much influenced by a family friend, the French geologist Jean-Étienne Guettard, and contributed to the latter's geologic and mineralogic atlas. In 1788 he presented a theory on geology to the Academy of Sciences.

When Lavoisier was but 23 he won a prize from the Academy for an essay on the lighting of cities. In 1768 he was elected to the Academy, an unusual honor for so young a man. The same year he was appointed to the *ferme générale*—a body of men who held the right to "farm" (collect) taxes. In 1776 Lavoisier began a career as director of the government arsenal.

The American colonies issued their Declaration of Independence in the same year, and soon colonial troops were using his improved gunpowder. By 1783 Lavoisier had solved what was the most significant chemical problem of the day by proving the connection between oxygen and fire. By brilliant experiments and delicate measurements, Lavoisier proved that burning, the rusting of metals, and the breathing of animals all consisted of the union of oxygen with other chemicals. Since this union, called oxidation, is one of the most important chemical processes, his discovery started the development of modern chemistry. He published his conclusions in 1789 in a work called *Traité élémentaire de chimie* (*Elementary Treatise on Chemistry*).

Lavoisier had become commissioner of weights and measures, and in 1791 he was appointed a commissary of the treasury. In 1794, however, the French revolutionists accused him and other members of the *ferme générale* of plotting to cheat the government. Because of this he was executed in Paris by the revolutionary tribunal on May 8, 1794.

LOUIS S. B. LEAKEY

(b. 1903–d. 1972)

Kenyan archaeologist and anthropologist Louis Seymour Bazett Leakey was born in Kabete, Kenya, on August 7, 1903. His fossil discoveries in East Africa proved that human beings were far older than had previously been believed and that human evolution was centered in Africa, rather than in Asia, as earlier discoveries had suggested. Leakey was also noted for his controversial interpretations of these archaeological finds.

Born of British missionary parents, Leakey spent his youth with the Kikuyu people of Kenya, about whom he later wrote. He was educated at the University of Cambridge and began his archaeological research in East Africa in 1924. He was later aided by his second wife, the archaeologist Mary Douglas Leakey (née Nicol), and their sons. He held various appointments at major British and American universities and was curator of the Coryndon Memorial Museum in Nairobi from 1945 to 1961.

In 1931 Leakey began his research at Olduvai Gorge in Tanzania, which became the site of his most famous discoveries. The first finds were animal fossils and crude stone tools, but in 1959 Mary Leakey uncovered a fossil hominin (member of the human lineage) that was given the name *Zinjanthropus* (now generally regarded as a form of *Paranthropus*, similar to *Australopithecus*) and was believed to be about 1.7 million years old. Leakey later theorized that *Zinjanthropus* was not a direct ancestor of modern man; he claimed this distinction for other hominin fossil remains that his team discovered at Olduvai Gorge in 1960–63 and that Leakey named *Homo habilis*. Leakey held that *H. habilis* lived contemporaneously with *Australopithecus* in East Africa and represented a more advanced hominin on the direct evolutionary line to *H. sapiens*. Initially many scientists disputed Leakey's interpretations and classifications of the fossils he had found, although they accepted the significance of the finds themselves. They contended that *H. habilis* was not sufficiently different from *Australopithecus* to justify a separate classification. Subsequent

Louis S. B. Leakey.

finds by the Leakey family and others, however, established that *H. habilis* does indeed represent an evolutionary step between the australopiths (who eventually became extinct) and *H. erectus*, who may have been a direct ancestor of modern man.

Among the other important finds made by Leakey's team was the discovery in 1948 at Rusinga Island in Lake Victoria, Kenya, of the remains of *Proconsul africanus*, a common ancestor of both humans and apes that lived about 25 million years ago. At Fort Ternan (east of Lake Victoria) in 1962, Leakey's team discovered the remains of *Kenyapithecus*, another link between apes and early man that lived about 14 million years ago.

The discoveries Leakey made formed the basis for the most important subsequent research into the earliest origins of human life. He was also instrumental in persuading Jane Goodall, Dian Fossey, and Biruté M. F. Galdikas to undertake their pioneering long-term studies of chimpanzees, gorillas, and orangutans in those animals' natural habitats. The Louis Leakey Memorial Institute for African Prehistory in Nairobi was founded by his son Richard Leakey as a fossil repository and postgraduate study center and laboratory.

Leakey wrote *Adam's Ancestors* (1934; revised edition, 1953), *Stone Age Africa* (1936), *White African* (1937), *Olduvai Gorge* (1951), *Mau Mau and the Kikuyu* (1952), *Olduvai Gorge, 1951–61* (1965), *Unveiling Man's Origins* (1969; with Vanne Morris Goodall), and *Animals of East Africa* (1969).

ANTON VAN LEEUWENHOEK

(b. 1632–d. 1723)

By means of his extraordinary ability to grind lenses, the Dutch microscopist Anton van Leeuwenhoek greatly improved the microscope as a scientific tool. This led to his doing a vast amount of innovative research on bacteria, protozoa, and other small life-forms that he called "animalcules" (tiny animals).

Leeuwenhoek was born in Delft, Holland, on October 24, 1632. He probably did not have much scientific education, for his family could not afford it. He first became a haberdasher and draper and, in 1660, chamberlain to the sheriffs at Delft. His hobby was lens grinding; and in his lifetime he ground about 400 lenses, most of which were quite small, with a magnifying power of from 50 to 300 times.

It was not only his lenses that made him world famous but also his work with the microscope. His keen powers of observation led to discoveries of major significance. For example, he observed and calculated the sizes of bacteria and protozoa and gave the first accurate description of red blood cells.

Although Leeuwenhoek lived in Delft, he maintained a regular correspondence with the Royal Society of England, to which he was elected in 1680. Most of his discoveries were published in the society's *Philosophical Transactions*. He continued his work throughout most of his 90 years. He died in Delft on August 26, 1723.

JUSTUS, BARON VON LIEBIG

(b. 1803–d. 1873)

Before Justus Liebig's time, chemistry was mainly theoretical and of interest only to scientists. Liebig helped to make chemistry useful in people's daily lives. His work with carbon compounds laid the foundations for modern organic chemistry.

Justus Liebig was born in Darmstadt, Germany, on May 12, 1803. He was the son of a paint dealer. Liebig began to learn chemistry as a boy when he first watched, then helped, his father improve paints. While serving as an apothecary's apprentice at 15, he read all the chemistry books he could find. Later he went to the University of Bonn, then transferred to the University of Erlangen. There he received a doctor's degree in 1822.

At 21 Liebig was invited to read his research report on fulminic acid to the French Academy of Sciences. The paper won praise and attention, and he gained the friendship of several important scientists. In 1824 Liebig was appointed to the University of Giessen, where he set up the first experimental laboratory for college students. He was made a baron in 1845. Liebig taught at Giessen until 1852, when he became a professor at the University of Munich. There he devoted himself to more literary activities, stressing broad applications of chemistry to human life. He died in Munich on April 18, 1873.

Liebig discovered chloral and chloroform, important contributions to medicine, and aldehyde, a chemical widely employed in industry. He improved methods for producing potassium cyanide, used in electroplating and in making ferrocyanides. Liebig's studies of meat juices resulted in meat extracts and special baby foods. With Friedrich Wöhler he did research on the benzol compounds and uric acid.

Liebig showed that the mineral and organic worlds are composed of the same elements. He showed that plants use elements from the soil for growth and pass them on to animals that eat the plants. His studies of soil led to the use of chemical fertilizers to replace minerals withdrawn by crops and to supply minerals lacking in some soils.

CAROLUS LINNAEUS
(b. 1707–d. 1778)

The Swedish naturalist and physician Linnaeus brought into general use the scientific system of classifying plants and animals that is now universally used. This is the binomial (two-name) system, in which each living thing is assigned a name consisting of two Latin words. The first word is the name of the genus and the second the species. So important was Linnaeus that he is called the Father of Systematic Botany.

Linnaeus was born Carl von Linné on May 23, 1707, in Rashult, Sweden. (In later years he preferred the latinized form of his name.) Although his father, a curate, wanted the boy to follow in his footsteps, Carl was interested in plants and animals. He was nicknamed "the little botanist" when he was 8 years old. The village physician saw that the boy had unusual gifts and encouraged the father to help care for Carl while he studied medicine at the University of Uppsala beginning in 1728.

There his talents soon won him an appointment as lecturer in botany. Later the Academy of Sciences of Uppsala sent him on a 5,000-mile (8,000-kilometer) botanical survey of Lapland. The scientific results of his journey were published in *Flora Lapponica* in 1737. His future wife, Sara Moraea, helped provide the funds with which he obtained his doctor's degree in medicine at a university in Holland.

In Holland Linnaeus became medical attendant to an Amsterdam banker who had a large botanical garden. Linnaeus was made director of this garden. In the next few years he published *Systema naturae* ("System of Nature") and *Genera plantarum* ("Species of Plants"). Into later editions of these he introduced his famous system of classification.

Carolus Linnaeus.

After scientific journeys to France and England Linnaeus returned to Stockholm to practice medicine. In 1742 he was appointed to the chair of botany at Uppsala, where he spent the rest of his active life. Students came to him from many countries and searched the Earth for specimens to contribute to his studies. Linnaeus died on January 10, 1778, in Uppsala.

Linnaeus's system of classification was an artificial one. He himself regarded it as a temporary convenience to be replaced by a natural system whenever the fundamental relationships of plants became known. In the 19th century the theory of evolution supplied some of the principles needed for a natural system, but the broad outlines of Linnaeus's system were retained.

CHARLES LYELL

(b. 1797–d. 1875)

The science of geology owes an enormous debt of gratitude to Sir Charles Lyell. It was he who, early in the 19th century, devised the theories, methods, and principles on which the modern science is based. His major contribution was proving that all features of the Earth's surface were produced by natural forces operating for long times. His strong arguments that the Earth's crust was the product of thousands of millions of years of activity did away with the need for unscientific explanations based on the biblical record or on intermittent natural catastrophes. Lyell's achievements in geology also laid the foundations for evolutionary biology, a field that was to be more fully developed by a young friend, Charles Darwin.

Charles Lyell was born in eastern Scotland on November 14, 1797, and raised near Southampton, England. He graduated from Oxford University in 1819 and went on to study law in London. He had, however, become an amateur geologist, and as the years passed he devoted more and more time to this pursuit. He made explorations in the British Isles, on the continent, and in the United States. In 1830 the first volume of his *Principles of Geology* was published. Eight years later he published *Elements of Geology*. Both works were hailed as pioneering studies by other scientists, and he was recognized as one of the most eminent scholars in his field. In 1848 he was knighted.

With the publication of Darwin's *Origin of Species* in 1859, the work of Lyell was overshadowed—even among his colleagues. Yet it was to Lyell that Darwin owed much of the information that was the basis of his own work. Lyell continued his studies and revisions of his books until his death in London on February 22, 1875. He was buried in Westminster Abbey.

MARCELLO MALPIGHI
(b. 1628–d. 1694)

The Italian physician and biologist Marcello Malpighi founded the sciences of microscopic anatomy and histology. For more than 40 years he used microscopes of his own making to study and describe animal tissue. Through these lenses he was able to see the specific subdivisions of such organs as the liver, spleen, brain, and kidney. His research provided a foundation for later advances in physiology, embryology, and practical medicine. During his lifetime, however, he was caught in a conflict between ancient and modern medicine. The envy of his colleagues led, in 1684, to the destruction of his home, papers, books, and apparatuses.

Malpighi was born in Crevalcore on March 10, 1628. In 1653 he was granted doctorates in both medicine and philosophy from the University of Bologna. He taught there until 1656, when he was invited to the University of Pisa. He returned to Bologna in 1659, but after three years took a post at the University of Messina in Sicily. By 1667 he was back in Bologna again. Malpighi's work aroused the interest of the Royal Society in London. In 1669 he was named an honorary member, and from then on all his papers were published in London.

After his work was destroyed, he was invited in 1691 to become personal physician to Pope Innocent XII in Rome as recognition for his work. He was named a count and elected to the College of Doctors of Medicine. Malpighi died in Rome on November 30, 1694.

LYNN MARGULIS

(b. 1938–d. 2011)

American biologist Lynn Margulis's serial endosymbiotic theory of eukaryotic cell development revolutionized the modern concept of how life arose on Earth. Margulis was born on March 5, 1938, and raised in Chicago. Intellectually precocious, she graduated with a bachelor's degree from the University of Chicago in 1957. Soon after, she married American astronomer Carl Sagan, with whom she had two children; one, Dorion, would become her frequent collaborator. The couple divorced in 1964. Margulis earned a master's degree in zoology and genetics from the University of Wisconsin at Madison in 1960 and a Ph.D. in genetics from the University of California, Berkeley, in 1965. She joined the biology department of Boston University in 1966 and taught there until 1988, when she was named distinguished university professor in the department of botany at the University of Massachusetts at Amherst. She retained that title when her affiliation at the university changed to the department of biology in 1993 and then to the department of geosciences in 1997.

Throughout most of her career, Margulis was considered a radical by peers who pursued traditional Darwinian "survival of the fittest" approaches to biology. Her ideas, which focused on symbiosis—a living arrangement of two different organisms in an association that can be either beneficial or unfavorable—were frequently greeted with skepticism and even hostility. Among her most important work was the development of the serial endosymbiotic theory (SET) of the origin of cells, which posits that eukaryotic cells (cells with nuclei) evolved from the symbiotic merger of bacteria without nuclei that had previously existed independently. In this theory, mitochondria and chloroplasts, two major organelles of eukaryotic cells, are descendants of once free-living bacterial species. She explained the concept in her first book, *Origin of Eukaryotic Cells* (1970). At the time, her theory was regarded as far-fetched, but it has since been widely accepted. She elaborated in her 1981 classic, *Symbiosis in Cell Evolution*, proposing that another symbiotic merger of cells with bacteria—this time spirochetes, a type of bacterium that undulates rapidly—developed into the internal transportation system of the nucleated cell. Margulis further postulated that eukaryotic cilia were also originally spirochetes and that cytoplasm evolved from a symbiotic relationship between eubacteria and archaebacteria.

Her 1982 book *Five Kingdoms*, written with American biologist Karlene V. Schwartz, articulates a five-kingdom system of classifying life on Earth—animals, plants, bacteria (prokaryotes), fungi, and protoctists. The protist kingdom, which comprises most unicellular organisms (and multicellular algae) in other systems, is rejected as too general. Many of the organisms usually categorized as protists are placed in one of the other four kingdoms; protoctists make up the remaining organisms, which are all aquatic, and include algae and slime molds. Margulis edited portions of the compendium *Handbook of Protoctista* (1990).

Another area of interest for Margulis was her long collaboration with British scientist James Lovelock on the controversial Gaia hypothesis. This proposes that the Earth can be viewed as a single self-regulating organism—that is, a complex entity whose living and inorganic elements are interdependent and whose life-forms actively modify the environment to maintain hospitable conditions.

In addition to Margulis's scholarly publications, she wrote numerous books interpreting scientific concepts and quandaries for a popular audience. Among them were *Mystery Dance: On the Evolution of Human Sexuality* (1991), *What Is Life?* (1995), *What Is Sex?* (1997), and *Dazzle Gradually: Reflections on Nature in Nature* (2007), all written with her son. She also wrote a book of stories, *Luminous Fish* (2007). Her later efforts were published under the Sciencewriters Books imprint of Chelsea Green Publishing, which she cofounded with Dorion in 2006.

Margulis was elected to the National Academy of Sciences in 1983 and was one of three American members of the Russian Academy of Natural Sciences. She was awarded the William Procter Prize of Sigma

Xi, an international research society, and the U.S. National Medal of Science in 1999. In 2008 she received the Darwin-Wallace Medal of the Linnean Society of London.

JAMES CLERK MAXWELL

(b. 1831–d. 1879)

Scientists of the Royal Society of Edinburgh must have been stunned to discover that the paper submitted to them in 1845 was the work of a 14-year-old boy. James Clerk Maxwell's first scientific paper, "On the Description of Oval Curves," marked the beginning of an impressive career in science.

Maxwell was born in Edinburgh, Scotland, on November 13, 1831. His family's original name was Clerk. "Maxwell" was added later. Maxwell's mother died when he was 8 years old. He was sent to Edinburgh Academy in 1841, and at 16 he entered the University of Edinburgh. In 1850 he went to the University of Cambridge. There he won honors and prizes in mathematics and became a lecturer at Trinity College. Maxwell obtained a mathematics degree in 1854. Two years later he joined the faculty of King's College, London. He retired in 1865 to carry on his experimental work but returned to Cambridge in 1871 to plan the famous Cavendish laboratory and was its first professor of physics.

Maxwell's theory of electromagnetic waves established him as one of the greatest scientists in history. He also contributed to the study of color blindness and color vision and the study of Saturn's rings. Maxwell's theory that the rings are composed of different masses of matter was confirmed 100 years later by the first Voyager space probe to reach Saturn. Although Maxwell did not originate the kinetic theory of gases, he was the first to apply methods of probability and statistics to describe the properties of gas molecules. Out of his investigation of the color theory came the first color photograph, which was produced by photographing one subject through filters of the three primary colors of light (red, green, and blue) and then recombining the images.

In his famous work with electricity and magnetism, he suggested that electromagnetism moved through space in waves that could be generated in the laboratory. By calculating their velocity he found that the speed of electromagnetic waves was the same as that of light waves. He concluded that light waves are electromagnetic in nature. At the time there was no evidence of comparable waves that could be transmitted or detected over any considerable distance.

Maxwell died in Cambridge on November 5, 1879, before this theory was successfully tested. In 1888 Heinrich Hertz performed experiments based on Maxwell's theories and demonstrated that an electric disturbance is transmitted through space in the form of waves. Today electromagnetic waves are known to cover a wide spectrum of radiation.

Maxwell expressed all the fundamental laws of light, electricity, and magnetism in a few mathematical equations, commonly called the Maxwell field equations. These equations were long considered a fundamental law of the universe, like Newton's laws of motion and gravitation. They do not apply, however, to phenomena that are governed by quantum theory, wave mechanics, and relativity.

BARBARA MCCLINTOCK

(b. 1902–d. 1992)

The American scientist Barbara McClintock's discovery in the 1940s and 1950s of mobile genetic elements, or "jumping genes," won her the Nobel Prize for physiology or medicine in 1983.

McClintock, whose father was a physician, took great pleasure in science as a child and evidenced early the independence of mind and action that she would exhibit throughout the rest of her life. After attending high school, she enrolled as a biology major at Cornell University in 1919. She received a B.S. in 1923, a master's degree two years later, and, having specialized in cytology, genetics, and zoology, a Ph.D. in 1927. During graduate school she began the work that would occupy her entire professional life: the chromosomal analysis of corn (maize). She used a microscope and a staining technique that allowed her to examine, identify, and describe individual corn chromosomes.

In 1931 she and a colleague, Harriet Creighton, published "A Correlation of Cytological and Genetical Crossing-over in *Zea mays*," a paper that established that chromosomes formed the basis of genetics. Based on her experiments and publications during the 1930s, McClintock was elected vice president of the Genetics Society of America in 1939 and president of the Genetics Society in 1944. She received a Guggenheim Fellowship in 1933 to study in Germany, but she left early because of the rise of Nazism. When she returned to Cornell, her alma mater, she found that the university would not hire a female professor. The Rockefeller Foundation funded her research at Cornell (1934–36) until she was hired by the University of Missouri (1936–41).

In 1941 McClintock moved to Long Island, New York, to work at the Cold Spring Harbor Laboratory, where she spent the rest of her professional life. In the 1940s, by observing and experimenting with variations in the coloration of kernels of corn, she discovered that genetic information is not stationary. By tracing pigmentation changes in corn and using a microscope to examine that plant's large chromosomes, she isolated two genes that she called controlling elements. These genes controlled the genes that were actually responsible for pigmentation. McClintock found that the controlling elements could move along the chromosome to a different site and that these changes affected the behavior of neighboring genes. She suggested that these transposable elements were responsible for new mutations in pigmentation or other characteristics.

McClintock's work was ahead of its time and was for many years considered too radical—or was simply ignored—by her fellow scientists. Deeply disappointed with her colleagues, she stopped publishing the results of her work and ceased giving lectures, though she continued doing research. Not until the late 1960s and 1970s, after biologists had determined that the genetic material was DNA, did members of the scientific community begin to verify her early findings. When recognition finally came, McClintock was inundated with awards and honors, most notably the 1983 Nobel Prize for physiology or medicine. She was the first woman to be the sole winner of this award.

LISE MEITNER

(b. 1878–d. 1968)

The Austrian physicist Lise Meitner shared the Enrico Fermi award in 1966 with Otto Hahn and Fritz Strassmann for research leading to the discovery of nuclear fission. Her own primary work in physics dealt with the relation between beta and gamma rays.

Meitner was born in Vienna on November 7, 1878. She studied at the University of Vienna, where she received her doctorate in physics in 1907. She then went to Berlin to join chemist Otto Hahn in research on radioactivity. She studied with Max Planck and worked as his assistant.

In 1913 Meitner became a member of the Kaiser Wilhelm Institute in Berlin (now the Max Planck Institute). In 1917 she became head of its physics section and codirector with Otto Hahn. They worked together for about 30 years and discovered and named protactinium. They also investigated the products of neutron bombardment of uranium.

Because she was Jewish, Meitner fled Germany in 1938 to escape Nazi persecution. She went to Sweden, which remained neutral during World War II. Here, with her nephew Otto Frisch, she studied the physical characteristics of neutron-bombarded uranium and proposed the name fission for the process. Hahn and Strassmann, following the same line of research, noted that the bombardment produced much lighter elements. Later advances in the study of nuclear fission led to nuclear weapons and nuclear power. In 1960 Meitner retired to live in England. She died in Cambridge on October 27, 1968.

CRAIG C. MELLO

(b. 1960–)

A merican scientist Craig C. Mello was a corecipient, with Andrew Z. Fire, of the Nobel Prize for physiology or medicine in 2006 for discovering RNA interference (RNAi), a mechanism that regulates gene activity. Mello was born in New Haven, Connecticut, and grew up in northern Virginia. As a young boy, he developed an intense curiosity in the living world. His curiosity was largely influenced by his father, James Mello, a paleontologist who had served as the associate director of the National Museum of Natural History at the Smithsonian Institution in Washington, D.C. Mello was intrigued by fundamental concepts such as evolution. He felt that these concepts encouraged humans to ask questions about the world around them, a belief that led to his rejection of religion at a young age.

Mello attended Brown University in Providence, Rhode Island, studying biochemistry and molecular biology and receiving a B.S. degree in 1982. He began his graduate studies in biology at the University of Colorado in Boulder, where he worked in the laboratory of American molecular biologist David Hirsh, who was investigating the nematode *Caenorhabditis elegans*. While conducting research in Hirsh's lab, Mello was introduced to American molecular biologist Dan Stinchcomb. When Stinchcomb decided to move to Harvard University in Cambridge, Massachusetts, to start his own research laboratory, Mello decided to follow him. At Harvard Mello became deeply involved in research on *C. elegans*, and his studies led him to American scientist Andrew Z. Fire, who was working at the Carnegie Institution for Science in Baltimore, Maryland. Both Mello and Fire were working to find a way to insert DNA into *C. elegans*, a process known as DNA transformation. After exchanging ideas and elaborating on one another's experiments, they successfully developed a procedure for DNA transformation in nematodes. In 1990, following the completion of his thesis, *C. elegans DNA Transformation*, Mello graduated from Harvard with a Ph.D. in biology.

Mello worked at the Fred Hutchinson Cancer Research Center in Seattle, Washington, from 1990 to 1994. He continued studying *C. elegans*, though his focus had shifted to identifying genes involved in regulating nematode development. In 1994 Mello joined the faculty at the University of Massachusetts Medical School. He became interested in an RNA injection technique used to silence genes. Silencing genes in *C. elegans* enabled Mello to identify the functions of the genes he had discovered while working in Seattle. He soon found that some nematode embryos that had been injected with RNA to silence certain genes were able to transmit the silencing effect to their offspring. Mello and Fire worked in collaboration to uncover the cellular mechanism driving this active silencing phenomenon and discovered that the genes were being silenced by double-stranded RNA. Known as RNAi, this mechanism regulates gene activity and helps defend against viral infection. In 1998 they published their findings, for which they later received the Nobel Prize. RNAi has proved a valuable research tool, enabling scientists to block genes in order to uncover the basic functions and roles of genes in disease. RNAi can also be used to develop new treatments for a number of diseases, including AIDS, cancer, and hepatitis. Following the RNAi publication, Mello focused his research on applying the silencing technique to the study of embryonic cell differentiation in *C. elegans*. In 2000 Mello was awarded the title of Howard Hughes Medical Investigator because of his significant contributions to science.

GREGOR MENDEL

(b. 1822–d. 1884)

The laws of heredity on which the modern science of genetics is based were discovered by an obscure Austrian monk named Gregor Mendel. Yet Mendel's discoveries remained virtually unknown for more than 30 years after he completed his experiments—in spite of the fact that his papers reached the largest libraries of Europe and the United States.

Johann Mendel was born on July 22, 1822, in Heinzendorf, Austria.

Gregor Mendel.

He took the name Gregor when he entered the monastery in Brünn, Moravia (now Brno, Czech Republic) in 1843. He studied for two years at the Philosophical Institute in Olmütz (now Olomouc, Czech Republic), before going to Brünn. He became a priest in 1847. For most of the next 20 years he taught at a nearby high school, except for two years of study at the University of Vienna (1851–53). In 1868 Mendel was elected abbot of the monastery.

Mendel's famous garden-pea experiments began in 1856 in the monastery garden. He proposed that the existence of characteristics such as blossom color is due to the occurrence of paired elementary units of heredity, now known as genes. Mendel presented his work to the local Natural Science Society in 1865 in a paper entitled "Experiments with Plant Hybrids." Administrative duties after 1868 kept him too busy for further research. He lived out his life in relative obscurity, dying on January 6, 1884. In 1900, independent research by other scientists confirmed Mendel's results.

DMITRY MENDELEYEV

(b. 1834–d. 1907)

The periodic table of the elements used in chemistry was devised by the Russian scientist Dmitry Mendeleyev (also spelled Dmitri Mendeleev). His final version of the table in 1871 left gaps, suggesting that other elements would later be discovered. He also predicted the characteristics of these unknown elements.

Dmitry Ivanovich Mendeleyev was born in Tobolsk, Siberia, on February 8, 1834. After his father's blindness and death in 1847, his mother operated a glass factory. When the factory was destroyed by fire, the family moved to Moscow and later to St. Petersburg, where Dmitry attended the Pedagogical Institute. He qualified as a teacher in 1855 and was sent south to Odessa to continue studies in chemistry. He received his first university post in 1857 and was sent to the University of Heidelberg (1859–61) for further study. Once back in

Dmitry Mendeleyev.

St. Petersburg he took up editing and scientific writing. He became a professor of chemistry at the Technical Institute in 1864. His textbook, *The Principles of Chemistry*, was published in 1868–70.

While writing the book he began to investigate the relationships between chemical elements. Out of this research came the periodic table that listed all of the elements by atomic weight and grouped them into related categories. Once the table was accepted, it became very useful in understanding the radioactive decay process by which one element is transformed into another.

Mendeleyev also made significant contributions to Russian industry and agriculture. Driven from teaching because of his progressive social views, his last years were spent as head of the Bureau of Weights and Measures. He died on February 2, 1907.

THOMAS HUNT MORGAN

(b. 1866–d. 1945)

The American zoologist and geneticist Thomas Hunt Morgan is famous for his experimental research with the fruit fly (*Drosophila*) by which he established the chromosome theory of heredity. He showed that genes are linked in a series on chromosomes and are responsible for identifiable, hereditary traits. Morgan's work played a key role in establishing the field of genetics. He received the Nobel Prize for physiology or medicine in 1933.

Early in life, Morgan showed an interest in natural history. In 1886 he received the B.S. degree from the State College of Kentucky (later the University of Kentucky) in zoology and then entered Johns Hopkins University for graduate work in biology.

Morgan apparently began breeding *Drosophila* in 1908. In 1909 he observed a small but discrete variation known as white-eye in a single male fly in one of his culture bottles. Aroused by curiosity, he bred the fly with normal (red-eyed) females. All of the offspring (F_1) were red-eyed. Brother–sister matings among the F_1 generation produced a second generation (F_2) with some white-eyed flies, all of which were males. To explain this curious phenomenon, Morgan developed the hypothesis of sex-limited—today called sex-linked—characters, which he postulated were part of the X chromosome of females. Other genetic variations arose in Morgan's stock, many of which were also found to be sex linked. Because all the sex-linked characters were usually inherited together, Morgan became convinced that the X chromosome carried a number of discrete hereditary units, or factors. He adopted the term gene, which was introduced by the Danish botanist Wilhelm Johannsen in 1909 and concluded that genes were possibly arranged in a linear fashion on chromosomes. Much to his credit, Morgan rejected his skepticism about both the Mendelian and chromosome theories when he saw from two independent lines of evidence—breeding experiments and cytology—that one could be treated in terms of the other.

In collaboration with A. H. Sturtevant, C. B. Bridges, and H. J. Muller, Morgan quickly developed the *Drosophila* work into a large-scale theory of heredity. Particularly important in this work was the demonstration that each Mendelian gene could be assigned a specific position along a linear chromosome "map." It was later shown that these map positions could be identified with precise chromosome regions, providing definitive proof that Mendel's factors had a physical basis in chromosome structure. A summary and presentation of the early phases of this work was published by Morgan, Sturtevant, Bridges, and Muller in 1915 as the influential book *The Mechanism of Mendelian Heredity*.

ISAAC NEWTON

(b. 1642–d. 1727)

The chief figure of the scientific revolution of the 17th century was Sir Isaac Newton. He was a physicist and mathematician who laid the foundations of calculus and extended the understanding of color and light. He also studied the mechanics of planetary orbits, formulated three fundamental laws of motion, and developed the law of gravitation, thus founding what is now known as classical mechanics. His work established the commonly held scientific view of the world until Albert Einstein published his theories of relativity in the early 20th century.

Isaac Newton was born on December 25, 1642, in Woolsthorpe, England. His father had died before he was born. Within a couple of years his mother remarried and sent him away to live with his grandmother. Newton was later sent to grammar school at Grantham to prepare for the university.

When Newton arrived at Trinity College, Cambridge, in 1661, he began studying the ancient teachings of Aristotle, as was then customary. Soon, however, he learned of the scientific revolution that had been going on in Europe through the work of Nicolaus Copernicus, Johannes Kepler, Galileo, and René Descartes. Newton became intrigued by the work of Descartes and other natural philosophers who—in contrast to Aristotle—viewed physical reality as composed entirely of particles of matter in motion. They held that all the phenomena of nature result from their mechanical interaction. In 1665 Newton graduated and returned to Woolsthorpe. There he continued his study of light, gravity, and mathematics that ultimately led him to three of the greatest discoveries in the history of science.

Newton's experiments with light showed that white light passed through a prism broke up into a wide color band, called a spectrum. Passed through another prism, the color band became white light again. Next he passed a single color through a prism. It remained unchanged. From this he concluded that white light is a mixture of pure colors. He also formulated the corpuscular theory of light, which states that light

Isaac Newton.

is made up of tiny particles, or corpuscles, traveling in straight lines at great speeds.

The law of gravitation arose from Newton's question: what keeps the Moon in its regular path around Earth? Newton concluded that an invisible force—gravity—acts between them, and he formulated a mathematical expression for the gravitational force. It states that every object in the universe attracts every other object with a force that operates through empty space. This force varies with the masses of the objects and the distance between them.

In mathematics, Newton used the concepts of time and infinity to calculate the slopes of curves and the areas under curves. He developed his "fluxional" method—later known as calculus—in 1669 but did not publish it until 1704.

Meanwhile, Newton had been appointed professor of mathematics at Cambridge in 1669. Three years later he invented the reflecting telescope. In 1687 he published his major work, *Principia* (*Philosophiae Naturalis Principia Mathematica*, or "Mathematical Principles of Natural Philosophy"). One of the fundamental works of modern science, it set forth the basic principles of classical mechanics concerning force, mass, and motion as well as the theory of gravitation.

Newton was elected to Parliament twice, as a representative of Cambridge. In 1696 he was appointed warden of the mint. At that time a complete recoinage and standardization of coins was taking place. When the project was completed in 1699, he was made master of the mint. He was elected president of the Royal Society in 1703 and was knighted in 1705. Newton died in London on March 20, 1727, and was the first scientist to be honored with burial in Westminster Abbey.

J. ROBERT OPPENHEIMER

(b. 1904–d. 1967)

The theoretical physicist J. Robert Oppenheimer was director of the laboratory in Los Alamos, New Mexico, where scientists working on the Manhattan Project in the mid-1940s developed the atomic bomb.

Julius Robert Oppenheimer was born in New York City on April 22, 1904. He graduated from Harvard University in 1925 and went to England to do research at Cambridge University's Cavendish Laboratory. In 1927 he received his doctorate from Göttingen University in Germany, where he met other prominent physicists such as Niels Bohr and P. A. M. Dirac.

Upon his return to the United States, he became a professor of physics at the University of California at Berkeley and California Institute of Technology. He explored the energy processes of subatomic particles and quantum theory.

J. Robert Oppenheimer.

In 1943 Oppenheimer selected the Los Alamos site for the laboratory. After the war he resigned his post, and from 1947 to 1966 he was director of Princeton's Institute for Advanced Study. In 1954, during the period of anti-Communist hysteria promoted by Senator Joseph R. McCarthy of Wisconsin, the federal Personnel Security Board withdrew his military security clearance. Oppenheimer thus became the worldwide symbol of the scientist who becomes the victim of a witch hunt while trying to solve the moral problems rising out of scientific discoveries. His clearance was reinstated by President Lyndon Johnson in 1963, and he was given the Enrico Fermi Award of the Atomic Energy Commission. On February 18, 1967, he died of throat cancer at Princeton.

LOUIS PASTEUR

(b. 1822–d. 1895)

The French chemist Louis Pasteur devoted his life to solving practical problems of industry, agriculture, and medicine. His discoveries have saved countless lives and created new wealth for the world. Among his discoveries are the pasteurization process and ways of preventing silkworm diseases, anthrax, chicken cholera, and rabies. Pasteur sought no profits from his discoveries, and he supported his family on his professor's salary or on a modest government allowance. In the laboratory he was a calm and exact worker; but once sure of his findings, he vigorously defended them. Pasteur was an ardent patriot, zealous in his ambition to make France great through science.

Louis Pasteur was born on December 27, 1822, in Dôle, France. His father was a tanner. In 1827 the family moved to nearby Arbois, where Louis went to school. He was a hard-working pupil but not an especially brilliant one.

When he was 17 Pasteur received a degree of bachelor of letters at the Collège Royal de Besançon. For the next three years he tutored younger students and prepared for the École Normale Supérieure, a noted teacher-training college in Paris. As part of his studies he investigated the crystallographic, chemical, and optical properties of various forms of tartaric acid. His work laid the foundations for later study of the geometry of chemical bonds. Pasteur's investigations soon brought him recognition and also an appointment as assistant to a professor of chemistry.

Pasteur received a doctor of science degree in 1847 and was appointed professor of chemistry at the University of Strasbourg. Here he met Marie Laurent, daughter of the rector of the university. They were married in 1849. Pasteur's wife shared his love for science. They had five children; three died in childhood.

In 1854 Pasteur became professor of chemistry and dean of the school of science (Faculté des Sciences) at the University of Lille. Hearing of Pasteur's ability, a local distiller came to him for help in controlling the process of making alcohol by fermenting beet sugar. Pasteur saw that fermentation was not a simple chemical reaction but took place only in the presence of living organisms. He learned that fermentation, putrefaction, infection, and souring are caused by germs, or microbes.

Pasteur published his first paper on the formation of lactic acid and its function in souring milk in 1857. Further studies developed the valuable technique of pasteurization. The same year he was appointed manager and director of scientific studies at his old school, the École Normale Supérieure. During the next several years he extended his studies into the germ theory. He spent much time proving to doubting scientists that germs do not originate spontaneously in matter but enter from the outside.

In 1865 Pasteur was asked to help the French silk industry, which was near ruin as a result of a mysterious disease that attacked the silkworms. After intensive research, he discovered that two diseases were involved, both caused by bacteria on the mulberry leaves that provided food for the worms. The diseases were transmitted through the eggs to the next generation of worms. Pasteur showed the silkworm breeders how to identify healthy eggs under the microscope, how to destroy diseased eggs and worms, and how to prevent formation of disease bacteria on the mulberry leaves.

At 45 Pasteur was struck by paralysis. For a time recovery was uncertain, and he was confined to bed for months. The attack left its mark; for the rest of his life, one foot dragged a little as he walked.

In 1877 Pasteur began to seek a cure for anthrax, a disease that killed cattle, sheep, and other farm animals. He drew on research he was conducting on another animal disease, chicken cholera. When he inoculated healthy chickens with weakened cultures of the cholera microbes, the chickens suffered only a mild sickness and were thereafter immune to the disease. Pasteur successfully applied this technique of immunization to the prevention of anthrax.

Many scientists challenged Pasteur's anthrax prevention claims, and Pasteur agreed to a dramatic test. Forty-eight sheep and a few cows and goats were gathered in a pasture near the town of Melun. Half the animals were first immunized with cultures of weakened anthrax microbes; then all were injected with strong cultures.

Within a few days, the untreated animals were dead; but the immunized animals showed no effect of the disease. The test verified Pasteur's results beyond all doubt. Later he proposed that all inoculation cultures be called vaccines and the inoculating technique, vaccination.

Human beings contract rabies (or hydrophobia) when they are bitten by a dog or another animal that is suffering from the disease. Rabies slowly destroys the central nervous system by attacking the spinal cord. Pasteur reasoned that it might be possible to immunize people after they had been bitten but before destruction of the spinal cord began. He took spinal cord tissues of animals that had died of rabies and dried them for varying periods of time. He then made inoculations of the tissues and injected them into another stricken animal. The first inoculation was from the driest, weakest culture, and each successive inoculation was stronger. After repeated failures, he finally succeeded in halting the development of rabies in an infected dog. The treatment required 14 inoculations.

Pasteur hesitated to try the remedy on humans. The decision was forced on him in 1885 when the mother of 9-year-old Joseph Meister begged Pasteur to save her son. The boy had been bitten 14 times by a rabid dog. Pasteur treated the child. The wounds healed and no trace of rabies appeared. Thus Joseph became the first person saved by Pasteur's treatment.

Pasteur had won many honors for his previous discoveries; now the world united to do him special homage. Thousands of people contributed funds to establish a great laboratory, the Pasteur Institute, where scientists conduct research on various diseases. Pasteur died near St-Cloud, France, on September 28, 1895.

LINUS PAULING

(b. 1901–d. 1994)

The first person to be awarded two unshared Nobel Prizes was the American chemist Linus Pauling. He won the Nobel Prize for chemistry in 1954 for his work on chemical bonds and molecular structure. The Nobel peace prize was given to him in 1962 for his campaign to stop the testing of nuclear weapons.

Linus Carl Pauling was born on February 28, 1901, in Portland, Oregon. He graduated from Oregon State Agricultural College (now Oregon State University) in 1922 with a degree in chemical engineering. He received a doctorate from the California Institute of Technology (Caltech) in 1925. For the next two years Pauling was in Europe studying atomic and quantum physics with leading scientists in Munich, Zürich, London, and Copenhagen. In 1927 he returned to Caltech as an assistant professor of chemistry. He became a full professor in 1931 and remained with the school until 1964. During World War II Pauling served with the Office of Scientific Research and Development for the federal government.

Pauling's early investigations into the structure of crystals led him to consider the nature of chemical bonds and the structure of molecules. Results of his early work were published in 1939 as *The Nature of the Chemical Bond, and the Structure of Molecules and Crystals*. He then turned to the far more complex molecules of amino acids and the peptide chains that make up proteins. While

Linus Pauling.

107

investigating protein molecules, he noticed a structural fault in the hemoglobin of people who had sickle-cell anemia, a hereditary disease. The fault caused some red blood cells to become sickle shaped. His studies showed that increasing the level of oxygen in arterial blood temporarily restored the hemoglobin to normal.

Pauling made public in 1961 a molecular model to explain anesthesia. He introduced new ideas for understanding the processes of memory. In 1965 he published a new theory of the atomic nucleus.

During the 1950s, with the increasing spread of nuclear weapons, Pauling became concerned about the hazards of radiation in the atmosphere. He published his views in a book, *No More War!*, in 1958, and soon thereafter he presented to the United Nations a petition signed by 11,021 scientists from all parts of the world urging an end to nuclear testing . In 1963, the year a nuclear test-ban treaty was concluded, he joined the staff of the Center for the Study of Democratic Institutions in Santa Barbara, California, to work on the problems of war and peace. He resigned from Caltech the next year. From 1967 to 1969, while at the center, he also taught at the University of California in Santa Barbara. In 1969 he joined the chemistry department of Stanford University, where he gained wide attention by endorsing the theory that large doses of vitamin C could prevent or cure the common cold and other diseases. He remained at Stanford until he retired in 1974. He died on August 19, 1994, in Big Sur, California.

MAX PLANCK

(b. 1858–d. 1947)

Awarded the Nobel Prize for physics in 1918, German physicist Max Planck is best remembered as the originator of the quantum theory. His work helped usher in a new era in theoretical physics and revolutionized the scientific community's understanding of atomic and subatomic processes.

Max Karl Ernst Ludwig Planck was born on April 23, 1858, in Kiel,

Germany. His father, a distinguished jurist and professor of law, taught at the University of Kiel. At the age of 9, Planck entered Munich's famous Maximilian Gymnasium, where a teacher, Hermann Müller, first stimulated his interest in physics and mathematics. Although Planck excelled in all subjects, he decided to pursue a career in physics over his other great love, music.

In 1874, Planck enrolled at the University of Munich but spent a year at the University of Berlin studying with physicists Hermann von Helmholtz and Gustav Robert Kirchhoff. He returned to Munich to work on the second law of thermodynamics and received his doctorate in 1879. The next year he became a lecturer at the University of Munich and in 1885 was appointed associate professor at Kiel. Four years later Planck received an appointment to the University of Berlin, where he soon was promoted to full professor of theoretical physics. He remained in Berlin until shortly before his death.

Planck's work on the second law of thermodynamics eventually led to his quantum theory formulations, now known as Planck's radiation law and Planck's constant (symbolized by h). Planck's radiation law is a mathematical relationship calculated to measure the radiation of energy by a blackbody, or perfectly radiating object. In formulating the law, Planck had to abandon one of his most cherished beliefs—that the second law of thermodynamics was an absolute law of nature. Instead, he had to accept the fact that the second law is a statistical law. In addition, Planck had to assume in his formulations that radiation is emitted, transmitted, and absorbed, not continuously but in discrete packets or quanta of energy.

He also introduced his constant h in his radiation law calculations. Planck's constant is the product of energy multiplied by time, a quantity called action, and is often defined as the elementary quantum of action. It is the fundamental physical constant used in mathematical calculations of quantum mechanics, which describes the behavior of particles and waves on the atomic scale.

Planck announced his findings in 1900, but it was years before the full consequences of his revolutionary quantum theory were recognized. Throughout his life, Planck made significant contributions

Max Planck.

to optics, thermodynamics and statistical mechanics, physical chemistry, and other fields. In 1930 he was elected president of the Kaiser Wilhelm Society, which was renamed the Max Planck Society after World War II. Though deeply opposed to the fascist regime of Adolf Hitler, Planck remained in Germany throughout the war. He died in Göttingen, Germany, on October 4, 1947.

JOSEPH PRIESTLEY

(b. 1733–d. 1804)

A clergyman who at one time was driven from his home because of his liberal politics, Joseph Priestley is remembered principally for his contributions to science. For his best-known accomplishment—the discovery of oxygen—he must share the credit with the Swedish chemist Carl Wilhelm Scheele, who is believed to have made the same discovery somewhat earlier. Priestley announced his find, however, to the French chemist Antoine-Laurent Lavoisier. Lavoisier, realizing that Priestley had isolated an important new element, named it and demonstrated its role in combustion.

Priestley was born on March 13, 1733, near Leeds, Yorkshire, England. He studied for the ministry at Daventry Academy in Northamptonshire, but his unorthodox religious ideas made it easier for him to make his living as a teacher than as a clergyman. He taught at Warrington Academy in Lancashire, where his emphasis on practical education contributed greatly to the school's success.

In addition to his discovery of oxygen and other gases, Priestley studied electricity and optics. His belief in personal liberty led him to support the French Revolution. He and his family had settled in Birmingham in 1779, but opposition to his unpopular views forced them to leave there in 1791. Three years later he and his wife left England to join their sons in the United States. They settled in Northumberland, Pennsylvania, where Priestley died on February 6, 1804.

STANLEY PRUSINER

(b. 1942–)

For his discovery of an entirely new class of pathogen, the prion, American physician and researcher Stanley Prusiner was awarded the 1997 Nobel Prize in physiology or medicine. Prions were found to be responsible for different types of dementia in humans and animals.

Stanley Prusiner was born on May 28, 1942, in Des Moines, Iowa. He attended the University of Pennsylvania and graduated in 1964. Four years later he earned his medical degree from the University of Pennsylvania's School of Medicine. He completed his internship at the University of California at San Francisco (UCSF) in 1969 and participated in a residency in neurology there from 1972 to 1974.

In 1974 Prusiner began a long career at UCSF, where he worked as a professor in the departments of neurology, biochemistry, and biophysics. In the 1970s he became involved with the University of California at Berkeley as well, and for most of his career he maintained professorships at both schools.

Prusiner's most important contribution to his field was the discovery of an entirely new class of infectious disease-causing agents, called prions. The story of Prusiner's discovery of these pathogens began in 1972, when one of his patients died of a type of dementia called Creutzfeldt-Jakob disease (CJD). At that time little was known about CJD other than that it could be transmitted through extracts of diseased brains. Prusiner set out to determine exactly what the infectious agent was and how it worked.

For ten years Prusiner and his team of researchers worked on this project. In 1982 they finally determined that the causative agent was a single cellular protein, which Prusiner dubbed a "proteinaceous infectious particle," or prion. Many scientists were skeptical of this discovery—they believed Prusiner had in fact misidentified some sort of virus. Prusiner took the skepticism in stride and began to investigate how prions were made. His goal was to find the gene that controlled the formation of the prion.

In 1984 Prusiner was surprised to learn that a gene common to all humans and animals was responsible for the creation of prions. This suggested that everyone carried prions in their bodies, a circumstance that seemed strange and unlikely given that most people do not suffer from dementia. Later, Prusiner solved this problem with the discovery that prions exist in two forms—as disease-causing agents and as normal proteins. The pathogenic prions could initiate a chain reaction in which normal prions become diseased as well. Over time, this chain reaction causes brain tissue damage.

It was found that prions were the pathogens responsible not only for CJD but also for scrapie (a disease affecting sheep), kuru (a disease of New Guinea's aboriginal people), Gerstmann-Straussler-Scheinker disease (a heritable disease of humans that typically occurs in midlife and affects the cerebellum, causing ataxia and other problems with coordination), and other types of dementia. In 1992 Prusiner's discoveries gained worldwide attention as bovine spongiform encephalopathy, commonly called mad cow disease, affected thousands of English cattle. Prions were found to be the causative agents of mad cow disease. Since consumption of infected beef was linked to CJD in humans, the epidemic of mad cow disease caused widespread alarm in the public.

In addition to the Nobel Prize, Prusiner received many other awards in his life, including the 1993 Gairdner Foundation Award for Outstanding Achievement in Medical Science, the 1994 Albert Lasker Award for Basic Medical Research and the 1994 Paul Ehrlich Prize.

PTOLEMY

(b. 100?–d. 170?)

Claudius Ptolemaeus, known as Ptolemy, was an eminent astronomer, mathematician, and geographer who lived in the 2nd century CE. He was of Greek descent but worked mostly in Alexandria, Egypt. In several fields his writings represent the greatest achievement of Greco-Roman science, particularly his Earth-centered model of the universe.

Almost nothing is known about Ptolemy's life except what can be inferred from his writings. He was born about 100 CE. His first major astronomical work, the *Almagest*, was completed about 150 CE and contains astronomical observations that Ptolemy had made over the preceding quarter of a century. The size and content of his subsequent writings suggests that he lived until about 170 CE.

In the *Almagest* Ptolemy lays out his argument that Earth is a stationary sphere at the center of a vastly larger celestial sphere that revolves at a perfectly uniform rate around Earth. The celestial sphere carries with it the stars, the planets, the Sun, and the Moon—thereby causing their daily risings and settings. Through the course of a year the Sun slowly traces out a great orbit, the ecliptic, against the rotation of the celestial sphere. The Moon and planets similarly travel backward—thus, the planets were also known as "wandering stars"—against the "fixed stars" found in the ecliptic. The basic assumption of the *Almagest* is that the apparently irregular movements of the heavenly bodies are actually combinations of regular, uniform, circular motions. The work also provided a catalog of 1,022 stars.

Ptolemy was primarily responsible for the Earth-centered cosmology that prevailed in the Islamic world and in medieval Europe. This was not due to the *Almagest* so much as a later treatise, *Planetary Hypotheses*. In this work he proposed what is now called the Ptolemaic system—a unified system in which each heavenly body is attached to its own sphere and the set of spheres nested so that it extends without gaps from Earth to the celestial sphere. The Ptolemaic system was the official dogma of western Christendom until the 1500s, when it was replaced by Nicolaus Copernicus's Sun-centered system.

How much of the *Almagest* is original is difficult to determine. Ptolemy credited Hipparchus with essential elements of his solar theory, as well as parts of his lunar theory, while denying that Hipparchus constructed planetary models.

Ptolemy published several books on new geometrical proofs and theorems, prepared a calendar that gave weather indications and the rising and setting of stars, wrote five books on optical phenomena, and developed a three-book treatise on music. His reputation as a geographer rests on his eight-volume work *Guide to Geography*. The books provide information on mapmaking and list places in Europe, Asia, and Africa by latitude and longitude. In spite of its many errors, this work greatly influenced succeeding generations of geographers and mapmakers.

ERNEST RUTHERFORD

(b. 1871–d. 1937)

One of the great pioneers in nuclear physics, Ernest Rutherford discovered radioactivity, explained the role of radioactive decay in the phenomenon of radioactivity, and proved that the positive electric charge in every atom is concentrated in a nucleus at the heart of the atom. Rutherford was also the first to transmute one chemical element into another by artificial means.

Ernest Rutherford was born near Nelson, New Zealand, on August 30, 1871. His father was a wheelwright. Ernest attended school in Nelson. In 1895 he won a scholarship to Cambridge University in England. His brilliance as a graduate student under Joseph J. Thomson won him a professorship of physics at McGill University in Montreal, Quebec, in 1898. In 1900 he returned to New Zealand to marry.

By 1902 Rutherford, in collaboration with Frederick Soddy, had succeeded in establishing a new branch of physics called radioactivity. He and Soddy published their findings on the properties of alpha and beta particles and on gamma-ray emission during radioactive decay. Their findings included the chain of decay from uranium through lighter elements. For this work Rutherford was awarded the Nobel Prize in chemistry in 1908.

In 1907 Rutherford accepted a post at Manchester University in England. By 1911, after studying the deflection of alpha particles shot through gold foil, he had established the nuclear theory of the atom. One of his students, Niels Bohr, used Rutherford's model of the atom to describe the hydrogen spectrum in terms of the quantum theory. Another student, Henry G. J. Moseley, used Rutherford's model, Bohr's theory, and his own X-ray diffraction studies to develop a new explanation of the periodic table of the elements in terms of atomic numbers.

During World War I Rutherford worked on methods of submarine detection. In April 1919 he succeeded Thomson as director of Cambridge University's Cavendish Laboratory. In June of that year Rutherford announced his success in artificially disintegrating nitrogen into hydrogen and oxygen by alpha particle bombardment. Rutherford then spent several years directing the development of proton accelerators (atom smashers). In 1932 John D. Cockcroft and E. T. S. Walton of Rutherford's group used the first workable atom smasher to artificially disintegrate lithium into helium.

Knighted in 1914, Rutherford was raised to the peerage as the first Baron Rutherford of Nelson in 1931—a barony that ceased to exist after his death. He also served as president of the Royal Society (1925–30) and as chairman of the Academic Assistance Council. He died at Cambridge on October 19, 1937, and was buried at Westminster Abbey, in London.

CARL SAGAN

(b. 1934–d. 1996)

The American astronomer Carl Sagan advanced the understanding of the origin of life in Earth's earliest atmosphere. He showed how adenosine triphosphate (ATP), a fundamental molecule that stores energy in all organisms, could have been produced from a mixture of basic organic molecules subjected to ultraviolet radiation or high-pressure shock waves. He worked from the principle that these molecules and sources of energy would have been present in high enough quantities to make this phenomenon possible. Sagan also studied the surface features and chemical atmospheres of all the other planets.

Carl Edward Sagan was born in Brooklyn, New York, on November 9, 1934. He earned a doctorate from the University of Chicago in 1960 and taught at the University of California at Berkeley and at Harvard University. He worked at the Smithsonian Astrophysical Observatory from 1962 to 1968. In 1966, working with James B. Pollack and Richard M. Goldstein, Sagan conducted radar studies of Mars that showed the existence of ridges.

Moving to Cornell University in 1968, he became director of the Laboratory of Planetary Studies and helped develop several unmanned space missions. Among his books are *Dragons of Eden* (1973), *Broca's Brain* (1979), *Contact* (1985), and *Shadows of Forgotten Ancestors* (1992). Sagan also coproduced and hosted the popular television series *Cosmos*. He died in Seattle, Washington, on December 20, 1996.

ABDUS SALAM
(b. 1926–d. 1996)

A long with Steven Weinberg and Sheldon Lee Glashow, Pakistani nuclear physicist Abdus Salam was the corecipient of the 1979 Nobel Prize for physics. The team won for their work in formulating the electroweak theory, which explains the unity of the weak nuclear force and electromagnetism.

Salam attended the Government College at Lahore, and in 1952 he received his Ph.D. in theoretical physics from the University of Cambridge. He returned to Pakistan as a professor of mathematics in 1951–54 and then went back to Cambridge as a lecturer in mathematics. He became professor of theoretical physics at the Imperial College of Science and Technology, London, in 1957. Salam was the first Pakistani and the first Muslim scientist to win a Nobel Prize. In 1964 he helped found the International Centre for Theoretical Physics at Trieste, Italy, in order to provide support for physicists from Third World countries. He served as the center's director until his death.

Salam carried out his Nobel Prize–winning research at the Imperial College of Science and Technology in the 1960s. His hypothetical equations, which demonstrated an underlying relationship between the electromagnetic force and the weak nuclear force, postulated that the weak force must be transmitted by hitherto-undiscovered particles known as weak vector bosons, or W and Z bosons. Weinberg and Glashow reached a similar conclusion using a different line of reasoning. The existence of the W and Z bosons was eventually verified in 1983 by researchers using particle accelerators at CERN.

FREDERICK SANGER

(b. 1918–d. 2013)

English biochemist Frederick Sanger was twice the recipient of the Nobel Prize for chemistry. He received the 1958 Nobel for his work on the structure of proteins, especially insulin, and he received his second Nobel in 1980 for research on deoxyribonucleic acid (DNA).

Sanger was born on August 13, 1918, in Rendcombe, Gloucestershire. Educated in England at the University of Cambridge, he thereafter worked principally at the British Medical Research Council in Cambridge (1951–83). Sanger spent 10 years elucidating the structure of the insulin molecule, determining the exact order of all its amino acids by 1955. His techniques for determining the order in which amino acids are linked in proteins made it possible to discover the structure of many other complex proteins.

Sanger later switched the focus of his research to DNA. Methods to determine the sequences of bases in DNA were pioneered in the 1970s by Sanger and the American molecular biologist Walter Gilbert. For his contributions to DNA sequencing methods, Sanger shared the 1980 Nobel with Gilbert and American biochemist Paul Berg; Sanger was only the fourth person ever to be awarded a second Nobel Prize.

Sanger's additional honors included election as a fellow of the Royal Society (1954), being named a Commander of the Order of the British Empire (1963), the Royal Society's Royal Medal (1969), the Royal Society's Copley Medal (1977), election to the Order of the Companions of Honour (1981), and the Order of Merit (1986). He retired in 1983. In 1992 the Wellcome Trust and the British Medical Research Council established a genome research center, honoring

Sanger by naming it the Wellcome Trust Sanger Institute. Sanger died on November 19, 2013, in Cambridge.

MATTHIAS SCHLEIDEN

(b. 1804–d. 1881)

The German botanist Matthias Jacob Schleiden (also spelled Matthias Jakob Schleiden) was the cofounder (with Theodor Schwann) of the cell theory. Schleiden was educated at Heidelberg (1824–27) and practiced law in Hamburg but soon developed his hobby of botany into a full-time pursuit. Repelled by contemporary botanists' emphasis on classification, Schleiden preferred to study plant structure under the microscope. While professor of botany at the University of Jena, he wrote "Contributions to Phytogenesis" (1838), in which he stated that the different parts of the plant organism are composed of cells or derivatives of cells. Thus, Schleiden became the first to formulate what was then an informal belief as a principle of biology equal in importance to the atomic theory of chemistry. He also recognized the importance of the cell nucleus, discovered in 1831 by the Scottish botanist Robert Brown, and sensed its connection with cell division. Schleiden was one of the first German biologists to accept Darwin's theory of evolution. He became professor of botany at Dorpat, Russia, in 1863.

ERWIN SCHRÖDINGER

(b. 1887–d. 1961)

The Austrian theoretical physicist Erwin Schrödinger contributed to the wave theory of matter and to other fundamentals of quantum mechanics. For new forms of atomic theory he shared the 1933 Nobel Prize for physics with the British physicist P. A. M. Dirac.

Schrödinger was born in Vienna, Austria, on August 12, 1887. He was educated at the University of Vienna and was subsequently professor of physics in Stuttgart, Germany; Breslau, Germany (now Wrocław, Poland); and Zürich, Switzerland. He succeeded Max Planck as professor of physics at the University of Berlin in 1927, and in 1940 he became a professor at the Dublin Institute for Advanced Studies in Ireland. In 1956 he retired and returned to Vienna, where he died on January 4, 1961.

His work in the fields of mathematical and atomic physics extended the ideas of Louis de Broglie. Niels Bohr had pictured the atom as consisting of a nucleus around which electrons rotated in fixed orbits. In the Bohr atom radiation was absorbed or emitted only when an electron changed from one orbit to another. The energy was absorbed or emitted in discrete packets. De Broglie's theory of wave mechanics, or matter waves, had modified this by supposing that a wave is associated with the electron circulating around the nucleus. Schrödinger extended these ideas by theorizing that such waves could be superimposed on each other. He thus related emission and absorption frequencies to the orbital frequencies. These ideas were confirmed by experimental observations. Schrödinger wrote several works on wave mechanics and also developed a new field theory.

THEODOR SCHWANN

(b. 1810–d. 1882)

The German physiologist Theodor Schwann founded modern histology, a branch of anatomy that deals with the minute structure of animal and plant tissues. He defined the cell as the basic unit of animal and plant structure.

Schwann was born on December 7, 1810, in Neuss, Prussia (now Germany). After studying medicine in Berlin, he assisted the physiologist Johannes Müller. In 1836, while investigating digestive processes, Schwann isolated a substance responsible for digestion in the stomach and named the substance pepsin. It was the first enzyme prepared from animal tissue. While professor of physiology at the University of Louvain in Belgium (1839–48), he observed the formation of yeast spores and concluded that the fermentation of sugar and starch was the result of life processes. He later extended the cell theory of animal structure to include plants and published his findings in 1839. From 1849 to 1879 Schwann taught at the universities of Louvain and Liège in Belgium.

Schwann also investigated muscular contraction and nerve structure. He discovered the striated muscle in the upper esophagus and the myelin sheath covering peripheral axons, which are now known as Schwann cells. Schwann also coined the term "metabolism" for the chemical changes that take place in living tissue, identified the role played by microorganisms in the decomposition of organic matter, and formulated the basic principles of embryology by observing that the egg is a single cell that eventually develops into a complete organism. Schwann died on January 11, 1882, in Cologne, Germany.

GEORGE GAYLORD SIMPSON

(b. 1902–d. 1984)

American paleontologist George Gaylord Simpson is known for his contributions to evolutionary theory and to the understanding of intercontinental migrations of animal species in past geological times.

Simpson received a doctorate from Yale University in 1926. In 1927 he joined the staff of the American Museum of Natural History, New York City, where he was to continue research in paleontology for three decades. The first 15 years were highly productive; he published about 150 scientific papers, many of considerable importance. A few dealt with lower vertebrates, but nearly all were on mammalian paleontology. He studied the Cretaceous mammals of Mongolia and North America, especially the Paleocene fauna of the latter continent (the Paleocene Epoch began about 65.5 million years ago and ended about 55.8 million years ago). This resulted in a major work on the Paleocene fauna of the Fort Union Formation of Montana, in which about 50 mammals of a variety of primitive types were found. The breadth of his studies of mammalian evolution led to the writing of a detailed classification of mammals that is standard in the field.

In the early Cenozoic a series of mammalian fauna lived in South America that were quite unlike those of any other continent. Those of the Neogene and Pleistocene forms were fairly well known, but little was known of the earlier history of the peculiar South American groups. Hence, in the early 1930s he made three expeditions to Patagonia to collect new material and restudy specimens already described; as a result of these efforts, the early history of the Neogene mammals of South America became vastly better known. He published several dozen papers on these forms in the late 1930s and afterward two volumes summarizing their early history.

During World War II Simpson did staff work for the U.S. Army, principally in North Africa. On his return to the American Museum, he became curator in charge of the active department of paleontology, as well as a professor at Columbia University. This restricted the time available for research, but his scientific productivity remained undiminished. While his descriptive work in paleontology continued, his interests spread to other fields. The possibility of applying mathematical methods to paleontology had already led to his coauthorship of a work on quantitative zoology. A consideration of the successive faunas of the various continental areas led to studies of the problems of the intercontinental migrations of animal species. Problems of taxonomy and classification are intimately connected with evolutionary studies, and, in addition to giving a thorough consideration of principles of classification in his work on mammalian classification, he published in 1961 a volume on *The Principles of Animal Taxonomy*. In a series of lectures which appeared in book form as *The Meaning of Evolution* in 1949, he discussed the philosophical implications of the acceptance of evolutionary theory, which attracted worldwide attention. In the postwar period there was a renewed study of evolutionary theory by geneticists, systematists, and paleontologists. Simpson took a major part in such studies; his principal publications in the area were his volumes *Tempo and Mode in Evolution* (1944) and *Major Features of Evolution* (1953).

EDWARD TELLER

(b. 1908–d. 2003)

The American physicist Edward Teller was a key figure in the development of nuclear weapons. He was instrumental in the research on the world's first hydrogen bomb.

He was born Ede Teller in Budapest, Hungary, on January 15, 1908. He received a doctorate in physical chemistry from the University of Leipzig and studied atomic physics with Niels Bohr in Copenhagen. In 1935 he accepted a post as visiting professor at George Washington University in Washington, D.C. By 1941 he had become a United States citizen and joined Enrico Fermi's research team in an experiment that produced the first controlled nuclear chain reaction.

In 1943 J. Robert Oppenheimer set up the Los Alamos Scientific Laboratory with the intent of designing an atomic fission bomb. Teller joined in the research, but he became increasingly intent on developing a thermonuclear hydrogen bomb that would be much more powerful than an atomic bomb. When two atomic bombs caused extreme destruction in Japan at the end of World War II, most Los Alamos scientists lost the desire to continue weapons research and thought that the creation of the even more devastating hydrogen bomb would be immoral. But Teller was convinced that developing advanced weapons would insure against future wars. When, in January 1950, Klaus Fuchs admitted that he had supplied the Soviet Union with information for making atomic bombs, the United States government gave Teller funds to develop the hydrogen bomb as quickly as possible. A finished bomb was detonated in the Pacific on November 1, 1952. Since then no thermonuclear weapons have been used in warfare, but many have been tested by various countries.

Another weapons laboratory was created in Livermore, California, with Teller in charge from 1958. He retired in 1960, and in the years that followed he continued research, became a spokesman for atomic affairs, and wrote several studies, including *Energy from Heaven and Earth*, published in 1979. In mid-2003 he was awarded the Presidential Medal of Freedom. Edward Teller died on September 9, 2003, in Stanford, California.

NIKOLA TESLA

(b. 1856–d. 1943)

The brilliant inventor and electrical engineer Nikola Tesla developed the alternating-current (AC) power system that provides electricity for homes and buildings. Tesla was granted more than 100 United States patents. Many of his discoveries led to electronic developments for which other scientists were honored.

Nikola Tesla was born in Smiljan, Croatia, then part of Austria-Hungary, on July 9 or 10, 1856. He was often sick during his boyhood, but he was a bright student with a photographic memory. Against his father's wishes he chose a career in electrical engineering. After his graduation from the University of Prague in 1880, Tesla worked as a telephone engineer in Budapest, Hungary. By 1882 he had devised an AC power system to replace the weak direct-current (DC) generators and motors then in use.

Tesla moved to the United States in 1884. Thomas Edison hired the young engineer as an assistant upon his arrival. Friction soon developed between the two, and by 1886 Tesla had lost his job. In 1887 he received enough money from backers to build a laboratory of his own in New York City.

Tesla became a United States citizen in 1891. A year earlier he had received a patent for his AC power system. At the heart of this system was the efficient polyphase induction motor that he developed. George Westinghouse bought the patent rights from Tesla. Westinghouse then launched the campaign that established alternating current as the prime electrical power supply in the United States.

Nikola Tesla.

Tesla later invented a high-frequency transformer, called the Tesla coil, which made AC power transmission practical. He also experimented with radio and designed an electronic tube for use as the detector in a voice radio system almost 20 years before Lee De Forest developed a similar device. Tesla lectured before large audiences of scientists in the United States and Europe between the years 1891 and 1893.

Although Tesla had laid the theoretical basis for radio communication as early as 1892, Guglielmo Marconi claimed all basic radio patents because of his own pioneering work in the field. In 1915 Tesla made an unsuccessful attempt to obtain a court injunction against the claims of Marconi. When the United States Supreme Court reviewed this decision in 1943, however, it reversed the decision and invalidated Marconi's patents on the ground that they had indeed been anticipated by earlier work.

In 1915 there was a report that Tesla and Edison had been chosen to share a Nobel Prize in physics. Although the report was later proven erroneous (neither had been nominated that year), one source said that Tesla declined his share of the award because of his doubt that Edison was a scientist in the strictest sense.

During his later years Tesla led a secluded, eccentric, and often destitute life, nearly forgotten by the world he believed would someday honor him. He died on January 7, 1943, in New York City. The Tesla Museum in Belgrade, Serbia, was dedicated to the inventor. In 1956 the tesla, a unit of magnetic flux density in the metric system, was named in his honor.

THALES OF MILETUS

(b. 624?–d. 546? BCE)

The Greek philosopher, astronomer, statesman, and mathematician Thales was renowned as one of the legendary Seven Wise Men (Sophoi) of antiquity. Thales is sometimes considered to be the first Greek philosopher because he was the first person to give a purely natural explanation of the origin of the world, free from any mythological aspects.

Thales was born in about 624 BCE in Miletus, an ancient seaport in

Asia Minor (modern Turkey). None of his writings has survived, but he was highly respected by learned Greeks. As a statesman, he advocated the federation of the Ionian cities of the Aegean region. As an astronomer, he advised navigators to steer by the Little Bear (Ursa Minor) rather than by the Great Bear (Ursa Major), both prominent constellations in the Northern Hemisphere. He also is said to have predicted a solar eclipse on May 28, 585 BCE, that stopped a battle in progress between King Alyattes of Lydia and King Cyaxares of Media.

Thales has been credited with the discovery of five theorems in geometry:

- that a circle is bisected by its diameter;
- that angles in a triangle opposite two sides of equal length are equal;
- that opposite angles formed by intersecting straight lines are equal;
- that any angle inscribed in a semicircle is a right angle;
- and that a triangle is determined if its base and the two angles at the base are given.

He reputedly applied his knowledge of geometry to measure the height of the Egyptian pyramids and to calculate the distance from shore of a ship at sea.

Thales is also remembered for his philosophical notion that water, or moisture, forms the fundamental building block of matter. He saw the Earth as a flat disc floating on a vast sea from which all things originated. To modern scholars, his choice of water as the essential substance is less important than his attempt to explain nature by referring to natural phenomena. Thales died in about 546 BCE.

J. J. THOMSON

(b. 1856–d. 1940)

The renowned British physicist Joseph J. Thomson was the discoverer of the electron. His research laid the foundation for developments of great importance in electricity, electronics, chemistry, and other sciences. He won the Nobel Prize for his work on the conduction of electricity through gases.

Thomson was born on December 18, 1856, in Cheetham, near Manchester, England. His father was a publisher and bookseller. Young Thomson planned to become an engineer, but while studying at Owens College he developed an intense interest in physics. He took advanced studies at Cambridge University, where he became a lecturer in 1882. Thomson published a treatise on vortex rings in 1883 that showed his early interest in the structure of the atom.

His work as a teacher and researcher impressed Cambridge authorities so favorably that he was appointed to the important Cavendish professorship of experimental physics when the chair became vacant in 1884. He soon gathered a brilliant group of students who also acted as research assistants. Seven of them later won Nobel Prizes. During this period Thomson was engaged chiefly in electromagnetic experiments.

In 1893 he published the results of these studies in *Notes on Recent Researches in Electricity and Magnetism*. He gave a course of lectures at Princeton University in 1896, summarizing his researches on the discharge of electricity through gases.

During 1896 he also conducted an investigation of cathode rays. On April 30, 1897, he startled the scientific world by announcing that the particles composing cathode rays were much smaller than atoms. These particles were later called electrons.

In his later researches Thomson found isotopes of the element neon and developed an electrical method for separating different kinds of atoms and molecules. He received the Nobel Prize in 1906. Among his other honors were a British knighthood, the Order of Merit, the Copley medal of the Royal Society, and honorary degrees from many universities. He was president of the Royal Society from 1915 to 1920. During World War I he served on the Admiralty Board of Invention and Research.

He married Rose Elizabeth Paget in 1890. They had a son, George, who became a noted physicist, and a daughter. Thomson died at Cambridge on August 30, 1940, and was buried in Westminster Abbey.

TYCHO BRAHE

(b. 1546–d. 1601)

The Danish astronomer Tycho Brahe was a pioneer in developing astronomical instruments and in measuring and fixing the positions of stars. His observations—the most accurate possible before the invention of the telescope—included a comprehensive study of the solar system and accurate positions of more than 777 fixed stars.

Tycho was born in the Scania region of Denmark on December 14, 1546. His education began with the study of law at the University of Copenhagen in 1559–62. Several important natural events turned Tycho from law to astronomy. The first was the total eclipse of the Sun predicted for August 21, 1560. Such a prediction seemed bold and marvelous to a 14-year-old student, but when Tycho witnessed its realization he saw and believed. His subsequent student life was divided between his daytime lectures on law, in response to the wishes of his uncle, and his nighttime vigil of the stars. The professor of mathematics helped him with the only printed astronomical book available, the *Almagest* of Ptolemy.

In 1562 Tycho's uncle sent him to the University of Leipzig, where he studied until 1565. Another significant event in Tycho's life occurred in August 1563, when he made his first recorded observation, a conjunction, or alignment, of Jupiter and Saturn. Almost immediately he found that the existing almanacs and ephemerides, which record the positions of stars and planets, were grossly inaccurate. The Copernican tables were several days off in predicting this event. In his youthful enthusiasm Tycho decided to devote his life to accumulating accurate observations of the heavens in order to correct the existing tables.

Between about 1565 and 1570 he traveled widely throughout Europe, studying and acquiring mathematical and astronomical instruments. Inheriting the estates of his father and an uncle, Tycho settled in Scania in about 1571 and built a small observatory. Here occurred the third and most important astronomical event in Tycho's life. On November 11, 1572, he suddenly saw a "new star," brighter than Venus and where no star was supposed to be, in the constellation Cassiopeia. He carefully observed the new star and showed that it lay beyond the Moon and therefore was in the realm of the fixed stars.

To the world at the time this was an alarming discovery because since ancient times the stars had been regarded as perfect and unchanging. The news that a star could change as dramatically as that described by Tycho, together with the reports of the Copernican theory that the Sun, not Earth, was the center of the universe, shook confidence in ancient knowledge. Tycho's discovery of the new star in 1572 and his publication of his observations in 1573 made him a respected astronomer throughout Europe.

The new star in the constellation Cassiopeia caused Tycho to rededicate himself to astronomy. King Frederick II of Denmark granted him an island and financial support to build a large observatory. Surrounded by scholars and visited by learned travelers from all over Europe, Tycho and his assistants collected observations and corrected nearly every known astronomical record.

After Frederick died in 1588, Tycho's influence dwindled and most of his financial support was stopped. Tycho left the observatory in 1597 and eventually settled in Prague. There he tried to continue his observations with the few instruments he had salvaged from the observatory. He was unable to recreate the spirit of active inquiry of his days in his observatory, however, and he died on October 24, 1601. He left all his observational data to Johannes Kepler, his pupil and assistant in the final years. With these data Kepler laid the groundwork for the work of Isaac Newton.

NEIL deGRASSE TYSON

(b. 1958–)

American astronomer Neil deGrasse Tyson has helped popularize science with his books and frequent appearances on radio and television. Tyson was born in New York City on October 5, 1958. When he was nine years old, his interest in astronomy was sparked by a trip to the Hayden Planetarium at the American Museum of Natural History in New York. Tyson received a bachelor's degree in physics from Har-

Neil deGrasse Tyson.

vard University in Cambridge, Massachusetts, in 1980 and a master's degree in astronomy from the University of Texas at Austin in 1983. He began writing a question-and-answer column for the University of Texas's popular astronomy magazine *StarDate*, and material from that column later appeared in his books *Merlin's Tour of the Universe* (1989) and *Just Visiting This Planet* (1998).

Tyson then earned a master's (1989) and a doctorate in astrophysics (1991) from Columbia University, in New York City. He was a postdoctoral research associate at Princeton University from 1991 to 1994, when he joined the Hayden Planetarium as a staff scientist. His research dealt with problems relating to galactic structure and evolution. He became acting director of the Hayden Planetarium in 1995 and director in 1996. From 1995 to 2005 he wrote monthly essays for *Natural History* magazine, some of which were collected in *Death by Black Hole: And Other Cosmic Quandaries* (2007), and in 2000 he wrote an autobiography, *The Sky Is Not the Limit: Adventures of an Urban Astrophysicist*.

As director of the Hayden Planetarium, Tyson oversaw a complete replacement of the facility, which opened in 2000. The new planetarium's exhibit categorized the solar system's bodies into groups. Pluto was not classified with either the terrestrial or Jovian planets but was grouped with the Kuiper belt objects. That decision (made six years before the International Astronomical Union designated Pluto as a dwarf planet) proved quite controversial, and Tyson was deluged with angry letters. He wrote about that experience in *The Pluto Files: The Rise and Fall of America's Favorite Planet* (2009), in which he attributed some of the sentimental attachment to Pluto's planethood to cultural factors such as Pluto being the only planet discovered by an American (astronomer Clyde Tombaugh) and having the popular cartoon character of Mickey Mouse's dog named after it.

Aside from his many books, Tyson was a well-known popularizer of science on television and radio. He appeared frequently on such talk shows as *The Daily Show with Jon Stewart* and *The Colbert Report*. In 2004 he was host of the four-episode television series *Origins*, which examined the origins of the universe, stars, planets, and life. From

2006 to 2011 he was the host of the television series *NOVA science-NOW*, and, beginning in 2009, he was also host of the weekly radio show *StarTalk*. From 2015 Tyson presided over a television talk show based on his radio program. It aired on the National Geographic Channel. In 2014 he hosted the television series *Cosmos: A Spacetime Odyssey*, a "continuation" (as he termed it) of astronomer Carl Sagan's popular series *Cosmos* (1980).

ANDREAS VESALIUS

(b. 1514–d. 1564)

The science of biology and the practice of medicine were revolutionized by the Flemish physician and surgeon Vesalius in the 16th century. By careful and painstaking dissections of cadavers he learned a great deal about the structure of the human body and laid the foundation for modern physiology.

Vesalius was born in December 1514 in Brussels into a family of physicians and pharmacists. He attended the University of Louvain (1529–33) and spent the next three years at the medical school of the University of Paris. In 1536 he returned home to spend another year at Louvain. He received his doctorate in medicine in 1537 and then worked in Padua as a lecturer in surgery. His anatomical studies led him to break with the theories of the Greek physician Galen, whose writings on physiology had long been considered authoritative. In 1543 Vesalius published his *Seven Books on the Structure of the Human Body*, the most accurate such work on the subject up to that time.

In the same year Vesalius presented a copy of his work to Emperor Charles V, who appointed him court physician. From 1553 to 1556 Vesalius was in Brussels, occupied with a flourishing medical practice. Three years later he went to Madrid to take up an appointment as physician to the court of Philip II. He remained in Madrid until 1564, when he was allowed to make a pilgrimage to Jerusalem. On the way back he became ill, and he died on the Greek island of Zacynthus in June 1564.

ALESSANDRO VOLTA

(b. 1745–d. 1827)

The Italian physicist Alessandro Volta is known for his invention of the electric battery, which provided the first source of continuous current. Volta, whose full name was Conte Alessandro Giuseppe Antonio Anastasio Volta, was born on February 18, 1745, in Como, Lombardy (in what is now Italy). He became professor of physics at the Royal School of Como in 1774. In 1775 his interest in electricity led him to improve the electrophorus, a device used to generate static electricity. He discovered and isolated methane gas in 1776. Three years later he was appointed to the chair of physics at the University of Pavia.

In 1791 Volta's friend Luigi Galvani announced that the contact of two different metals with the muscle of a frog resulted in the generation of an electric current. Galvani interpreted that as a new form of electricity found in living tissue, which he called "animal electricity." Volta felt that the frog merely conducted a current that flowed between the two metals, which he called "metallic electricity." He began experimenting in 1792 with metals alone. (He would detect the weak flow of electricity between disks of different metals by placing them on his tongue.) Volta found that animal tissue was not needed to produce a current. That provoked controversy between the animal-electricity adherents and the metallic-electricity advocates, but, with his announcement of the first electric battery in 1800, victory was assured for Volta.

Known as the voltaic pile or the voltaic column, Volta's battery consisted of alternating disks of zinc and silver (or copper and pewter) separated by paper or cloth soaked either in salt water or sodium hydroxide. A simple and reliable source of electric current that did not need to be recharged like the Leyden jar, his invention quickly led to a new wave of electrical experiments. Within six weeks of Volta's announcement, English scientists William Nicholson and Anthony Carlisle used a voltaic pile to decompose water into hydrogen and oxygen, thus discovering electrolysis (how an electric current leads to a chemical reaction) and creating the field of electrochemistry.

In 1801 in Paris Volta gave a demonstration of his battery's generation of electric current before Napoleon, who made Volta a count and a senator of the kingdom of Lombardy. Austrian Emperor Francis I made him director of the philosophical faculty at the University of Padua in 1815. The volt, a unit of the electromotive force that drives current, was named in his honor in 1881.

JAMES DEWEY WATSON

(b. 1928–)

American geneticist and biophysicist James Dewey Watson played a significant role in the discovery of the molecular structure of deoxyribonucleic acid (DNA)—the substance that is the basis of heredity. For this accomplishment he was awarded the 1962 Nobel Prize for physiology or medicine with Francis Crick and Maurice Wilkins.

Watson was born on April 6, 1928, in Chicago, Illinois. He enrolled at the University of Chicago when only 15 years old and graduated in 1947. In 1950 he received a doctorate from Indiana University, where he did research on viruses. Watson began his working career at the University of Copenhagen in Denmark, where he first decided to investigate DNA.

From 1951 to 1953 Watson did research at the Cavendish Laboratory at the University of Cambridge in England. There he learned X-ray diffraction, a technique that allows scientists to look at the structures of different materials. He also met Crick and worked with him on the problem of DNA structure. In the spring of 1953, Watson saw that the essential DNA components must be linked in definite pairs. This discovery was the key factor that enabled Watson and Crick to formulate a molecular model for DNA—a double helix, which can be pictured as a spiraling staircase or a twisting ladder. Watson and Crick's model also shows how the DNA molecule could duplicate itself. Thus, it became known how genes, and eventually chromosomes, duplicate themselves.

The pair's research answered one of the fundamental questions in genetics and led to their being awarded the Nobel Prize. They shared the award with Wilkins for his work in developing X-ray diffraction.

Watson taught at Harvard University in Cambridge, Massachusetts, from 1955 to 1976, serving as professor of biology from 1961. He conducted research on the role of nucleic acids in the synthesis of proteins. In 1965 he published *Molecular Biology of the Gene*, one of the most extensively used modern biology texts. He later wrote *The Double Helix* (1968), an informal account of the DNA discovery. In 1968 Watson assumed the leadership of the Laboratory of Quantitative Biology at Cold Spring Harbor, Long Island, New York, and made it a world center for research in molecular biology. He concentrated its efforts on cancer research. In 1981 his *The DNA Story* (written with John Tooze) was published.

From 1988 to 1992 at the National Institutes of Health, Watson helped direct the Human Genome Project. This project set out to map and decipher all the genes in the human chromosomes. In early 2007 Watson's own genome was sequenced and made available on the Internet. He was the second person in history to have a personal genome sequenced in its entirety. Watson retired at the end of 2007.

ALFRED WEGENER

(b. 1880–d. 1930)

In 1912 the German meteorologist Alfred Wegener proposed that throughout most of geologic time there was only one continental mass, which he named Pangaea (or "All-earth") and one ocean, called Panthalassa (or "All-sea"). His theory is known as the continental-drift theory. Bringing together a large mass of geologic and paleontological data, Wegener suggested that Pangaea fragmented during the Jurassic Period, and the parts began to move away from one another.

Alfred Lothar Wegener was born in Berlin, Germany, on November 1, 1880. The son of a director of an orphanage, he received his doctorate in astronomy from the University of Berlin in 1905. During this time he became interested in meteorology and geology. Wegener went on four expeditions to Greenland and was considered a specialist on the territory. From 1908 to 1912 he lectured at the Physical Institute in Marburg. He also suggested that lunar craters arose through meteoric bombardment rather than volcanic activity. His "continental-displacement" theory, published in 1915, stirred an international controversy from 1919 to 1928. Wegener died during his last Greenland expedition in November 1930. His theory was revived 20 years later with the development of the new science of paleomagnetism.

STEVEN WEINBERG

(b. 1933–)

In 1979 the American nuclear physicist Steven Weinberg shared the Nobel Prize for Physics with Sheldon Lee Glashow and Abdus Salam for work in formulating the electroweak theory, which explains the unity of electromagnetism with the weak nuclear force.

Weinberg and Glashow were members of the same classes at the Bronx High School of Science, New York City (1950), and Cornell University (1954). Weinberg went from Cornell to the Institute for Theoretical Physics (later known as the Niels Bohr Institute) at the University of Copenhagen for a year. He then obtained his doctorate at Princeton University in 1957.

Weinberg proposed his version of the electroweak theory in 1967. Electromagnetism and the weak force were both known to operate by the interchange of subatomic particles. Electromagnetism can operate at potentially infinite distances by means of massless particles called photons, while the weak force operates only at subatomic distances by means of massive particles called bosons. Weinberg was able to show that despite their apparent dissimilarities, photons and bosons are actually members of the same family of particles. His work, along with that of Glashow and Salam, made it possible to predict the outcome of new experiments in which elementary particles are made to impinge on one another. An important series of experiments in 1982–83 found strong evidence for the W and Z particles predicted by these scientists' electroweak theory.

Weinberg conducted research at Columbia University and at the Lawrence Berkeley Laboratory before joining the faculty of the University of California at Berkeley (1960–69). During his last years there, he also was a Morris Loeb Lecturer (1966–67) at Harvard—a post he held on several subsequent occasions as well—and a visiting professor (1968–69) at the Massachusetts Institute of Technology; he joined the latter faculty in 1969 and moved to Harvard University in 1973 and to the University of Texas at Austin in 1983.

EDWARD O. WILSON

(b. 1929–)

American biologist Edward O. Wilson is recognized as the world's leading authority on ants. He was also the foremost proponent of sociobiology, the study of the genetic basis of the social behavior of all animals, including humans.

Edward Osborne Wilson was born June 10, 1929, in Birmingham, Alabama. He received early training in biology at the University of Alabama (B.S., 1949; M.S., 1950). He received a doctorate in biology at Harvard University in 1955. After his appointment to Harvard in 1956, Wilson made a series of important discoveries, including the determination that ants communicate primarily through the transmission of chemical substances known as pheromones. In the course of revising the classification of ants native to the South Pacific, he formulated the concept of the "taxon cycle," in which speciation and species dispersal are linked to the varying habitats that organisms encounter as their populations expand. In 1971 he published *The Insect Societies*, his definitive work on ants and other social insects. The book provided a comprehensive picture of the ecology, population dynamics, and social behavior of thousands of species.

In Wilson's second major work, *Sociobiology: The New Synthesis* (1975), a treatment of the biological basis of social behavior, he proposed that the essentially biological principles on which animal societies are based also apply to humans. This thesis provoked condemnation from prominent researchers and scholars in a broad range of disciplines, who regarded it as an attempt to justify harmful or destructive behavior and unjust social relations in human societies. In fact, however, Wilson maintained that as little as 10 percent of human behavior is genetically induced, the rest being attributable to environment.

One of Wilson's most notable theories was that even a characteristic such as altruism may have evolved through natural selection. Traditionally, natural selection was thought to foster only those physical and behavioral traits that increase an individual's chances of reproducing. Thus, altruistic behavior—as when an organism sacrifices itself in order to save other members of its immediate family—would seem incompatible with this process. In *Sociobiology* Wilson argued that the sacrifice involved in much altruistic behavior results in saving closely related individuals—i.e., individuals who share many of the sacrificed organism's genes. Therefore, the preservation of the gene, rather than the preservation of the individual, was viewed as the focus of evolutionary strategy; the theory was known as kin selection. In later years, however, Wilson was inclined to think that highly social organisms are integrated to such an extent that they are better treated as one overall unit—a superorganism—rather than as individuals in their own right. This view was suggested by Charles Darwin himself in *On the Origin of Species* (1859). Wilson expounded on it in *Success, Dominance, and the Superorganism: The Case of the Social Insects* (1997).

EDWARD WITTEN

(b. 1951–)

A merican mathematical physicist Edward Witten was awarded the Fields Medal in 1990 for his work in superstring theory. He also received the Dirac Medal from the International Centre for Theoretical Physics (1985).

Witten was born on August 26, 1951, in Baltimore, Maryland, and educated at Brandeis University (B.A., 1971) in Waltham, Massachusetts, and Princeton University (M.A., 1974; Ph.D., 1976) in New Jersey. He held a fellowship at Harvard University (1976–77), was a junior fellow in the Harvard Society of Fellows (1977–80), and held a MacArthur Foundation fellowship (1982). He held an appointment at Princeton (1980–87) before moving to the Institute for Advanced Study, Princeton, in 1987.

Witten was awarded the Fields Medal at the International Congress of Mathematicians in Kyōto, Japan, in 1990. His early research interests were in electromagnetism, but he soon developed an interest in what is now known as superstring theory in mathematical physics. He made significant contributions to Morse theory, supersymmetry, and knot theory. Additionally, he explored the relationship between quantum field theory and the differential topology of manifolds of two and three dimensions. With the physicist Nathan Seiberg he produced a family of partial differential equations that greatly simplified Simon Donaldson's approach to the classification of four-dimensional manifolds.

Witten's publications include, with Sam B. Treimen, Roman Jackiw, and Bruno Zumino, *Current Algebra and Anomalies* (1985) and, with Michael B. Green and John H. Schwarz, *Superstring Theory* (1987).

CHIEN-SHIUNG WU

(b. 1912–d. 1997)

The Chinese-born physicist Chien-shiung Wu provided the first experimental proof that the principle of parity conservation does not hold in weak subatomic interactions.

Wu was born on May 31, 1912, in Liuho, Jiangsu Province. She went to the United States in 1936 to study at the University of California in Berkeley. After receiving her doctorate in 1940, she taught at Smith College, in Northampton, Massachusetts, and at Princeton University, in Princeton, New Jersey. In 1944 she worked on radiation detection in the Division of War Research at Columbia University, in New York City, and became professor of physics in 1957.

Chien-shiung Wu.

After the early 1930s conservation of parity, or symmetry, became a fundamental theory in quantum mechanics. In 1956 the theoretical physicists Tsung-Dao Lee and Chen Ning Yang proposed that parity is not conserved for one of the three basic nuclear interactions—weak interactions, which govern radioactive decay. In 1957 Wu proved them right by showing that the beta particles given off by cobalt-60 atoms have a preferred direction. Wu and others confirmed the conservation of vector current in nuclear beta decay in 1963. She also studied the structure of hemoglobin. Wu received the National Medal of Science in 1975 and served as president of the American Physical Society in 1975. She died in New York City on February 16, 1997.

SHINYA YAMANAKA

(b. 1962–)

Japanese physician and researcher Shinya Yamanaka developed a revolutionary method for generating stem cells from existing cells of the body. This method involved inserting specific genes into the nuclei of adult cells (e.g., connective-tissue cells), a process that resulted in the reversion of cells from an adult state to a pluripotent state. As pluripotent cells, they had regained the capacity to differentiate into any cell type of the body. Thus, the reverted cells became known as induced pluripotent stem (iPS) cells. Yamanaka and British developmental biologist John B. Gurdon shared the 2012 Nobel Prize for physiology or medicine for the discovery that mature cells could be reprogrammed.

Yamanaka received an M.D. from Kōbe University in 1987 and a Ph.D. in pharmacology from the Ōsaka City University Graduate School in 1993. That year he joined the Gladstone Institute of Cardiovascular Disease, San Francisco, where he began investigating the *c-Myc* gene in different strains of knockout mice (mice in which a specific gene has been rendered nonfunctional in order to investigate the gene's function). In 1996 Yamanaka returned to Ōsaka City University, where he remained until 1999, when he took a position at the Nara Institute of Science and Technology. During this period his research became increasingly focused on stem cells. In 2004 he moved to the Institute for Frontier Medical Sciences at Kyōto University, where he began his landmark studies on finding ways to induce pluripotency in cells. Yamanaka again sought research opportunities in the United States and subsequently was awarded funding that allowed him to split his time between Kyōto and the Gladstone Institute of Cardiovascular Disease. Yamanaka became a senior investigator at the Gladstone Institute in 2007.

In 2006 Yamanaka announced that he had succeeded in generating iPS cells. The cells had the properties of embryonic stem cells but were produced by inserting four specific genes into the nuclei of mouse adult fibroblasts (connective-tissue cells). The following year Yamanaka reported that he had derived iPS cells from human adult fibroblasts—the first successful attempt at generating human versions of these cells. This discovery marked a turning point in stem-cell research because it offered a way of obtaining human stem cells without the controversial use of human embryos. Yamanaka's technique to convert adult cells into iPS cells up to that time had employed a retrovirus that contained the *c-Myc* gene. This gene was believed to play a fundamental role in reprogramming the nuclei of adult cells. However, Yamanaka recognized that the activation of *c-Myc* during the process of creating iPS cells led to the formation of tumours when the stem cells were later transplanted into mice. He subsequently created iPS cells without *c-Myc* in order to render the cells noncancerous and thereby overcome a major concern in the therapeutic safety of iPS cells. In 2008 Yamanaka reported another breakthrough—the generation of iPS cells from mouse liver and stomach cells.

Yamanaka received multiple awards for his contributions to stem-cell research, including the Robert Koch Prize (2008), the Shaw Prize in Life Science and Medicine (2008), the Gairdner Foundation International Award (2009), the Albert Lasker Basic Medical Research Award (2009), and the Millennium Technology Prize (2012).

CHEN NING YANG

(b. 1922–)

A Chinese-born American theoretical physicist, Chen Ning Yang carried out research in particle physics with Tsung-Dao Lee that earned the two scientists the 1957 Nobel Prize for physics. Their work demonstrated that parity—the symmetry between physical phenomena occurring in right-handed and left-handed coordinate systems—is violated when elementary particles decay. Up until this discovery physicists had assumed that parity symmetry was a universal law.

Chen Ning Yang was born on September 22, 1922, in Hofei, China. Inspired by Benjamin Franklin's autobiography, he adopted the statesman's last name as his first name and became known as Frank Yang. In the United States he studied with Edward Teller and earned his Ph.D. in nuclear physics at the University of Chicago. While he was an assistant to Enrico Fermi, he and Lee began their collaboration. Their parity experiments also showed that the symmetry between particle and antiparticle, known as charge conjugation symmetry, is broken during the weak decays.

Yang became a professor at the Institute for Advanced Study in Princeton, New Jersey, in 1955. He became a United States citizen in 1964. From 1965 he was Albert Einstein professor at the Institute of Science, State University of New York at Stony Brook, Long Island. He received the Einstein Award in 1957 and the Rumford Prize in 1980.

YUKAWA HIDEKI

(b. 1907–d. 1981)

One of the most influential theoretical physicists of the 20th century, Yukawa Hideki was awarded the Nobel Prize for physics in 1949 for his meson theory of nuclear forces. He thus became Japan's first Nobel laureate at a time when Japanese scientific prestige was low.

Yukawa was born in Tokyo on January 23, 1907. His father, Takuji Ogawa, was a geologist and professor at Kyōto University, where Yukawa received his formal education. After graduating in 1929, Yukawa married Sumi Yukawa and assumed her family name. He lectured at Kyōto University for three years and in 1933 left to become a lecturer at Osaka Imperial University, earning his doctorate there in 1938. He returned to Kyōto University as lecturer in theoretical physics from 1939 until 1950.

In 1948, at the invitation of J. Robert Oppenheimer, Yukawa became a visiting professor at the Institute for Advanced Studies in Princeton, New Jersey, and from 1949 to 1953 he was a professor at Columbia University in New York City. As an expression of gratitude for Yukawa's scientific achievements and in order to persuade him to return to Japan, the Research Institute for

Fundamental Physics was established in Kyōto in 1953. Yukawa served as its director until his retirement in 1970. Yukawa wrote many essays on creativity and on the history and philosophy of science. He died in Kyōto on September 8, 1981.

Yukawa developed his meson theory in the 1930s. After a series of discoveries in 1932, physicists still could not explain why the positively charged protons in the atom's nucleus do not repel one another, causing the nucleus to split apart. Because two positively charged particles should repel one another, Yukawa believed that some other force must hold them together. This nuclear binding force, which is much stronger than the electrical repulsions between the protons in the nucleus, is now aptly named the strong force.

Only three subatomic particles—protons, neutrons, and electrons—were then known. In 1935 Yukawa predicted the existence of a new particle, now known as a pi-meson, or pion, with a mass between that of an electron and a proton. He proposed that the strong force is mediated by the exchange of pions between protons and neutrons in the nucleus. The existence of the pion was confirmed in 1947. Numerous other types of mesons have since been identified. Yukawa's work supported the earlier work of Werner Heisenberg and Enrico Fermi. It was a major contribution to nuclear and particle physics and to the continuing development of the theory of the strong force. (It is now thought that, at a deeper structural level, the exchange of particles called gluons between particles called quarks within the protons and neutrons is fundamental to the strong force.)

GLOSSARY

ALKALI A substance (as a hydroxide) that has a bitter taste and neutralizes acids.

AXON The long part of a neuron, or nervous system cell, that carries impulses away from the cell body.

CHROMOSOME One of the rod-shaped or threadlike DNA-containing bodies of a cell nucleus that contain all or most of the genes of an organism and can be seen especially during cell division.

COSMOLOGY A branch of astronomy that deals with the beginning, structure, and space-time relationships of the universe.

ECLIPTIC The great circle of the celestial sphere on which the Sun appears to move among the stars.

ELECTRODYNAMICS A branch of physics that deals with the effects arising from the interactions of electric currents with magnets, with other currents, or with themselves.

FERMENTATION The chemical breaking down of a substance (as in the souring of milk or the formation of alcohol from sugar) produced by an enzyme and often accompanied by the formation of a gas.

GENE A specific sequence of nucleotides in DNA or sometimes RNA that is usually located on a chromosome and that is the functional unit of inheritance controlling the transmission and expression of one or more traits by specifying the structure of a particular protein or by controlling the function of other genetic material.

HYDROSTATICS A branch of physics that deals with the characteristics of fluids at rest.

INOCULATION Introducing material (as a vaccine) into the body especially by injection to protect against or treat a disease.

METAPHYSICS The part of philosophy concerned with the ultimate causes and basic nature of things.

MITOCHONDRION Any of various round or long cellular organelles that are located in the cytoplasm outside the nucleus, produce energy for the cell through metabolic processes utilizing oxygen, and are rich in fats, proteins, and enzymes.

MORPHOLOGY A branch of biology that deals with the form and structure of animals and plants.

NUCLEAR FISSION The splitting of an atomic nucleus resulting in the release of large amounts of energy.

NUCLEUS A central point, group, or mass of something. In particular, 1) the central part of an atom that includes nearly all of the atomic mass and consists of protons and usually neutrons; or 2) a cell part that is characteristic of all living things with the exception of viruses, bacteria, and blue-green algae, that is necessary for heredity and for making proteins, that contains the chromosomes, and that is enclosed in a nuclear membrane.

OPTICS A science that deals with the nature and properties of light and the effects that it undergoes and produces.

ORGANIC Of, relating to, or obtained from living things.

OSCILLATION Swinging backward and forward like a pendulum.

PHENOMENON A fact, feature, or event of scientific interest. The plural of phenomenon is phenomena.

PHYSIOLOGY A branch of biology dealing with the processes and activities by which life is carried on and which are special features of the functioning of living things, tissues, and cells.

PROTOZOA A group of microorganisms (as amoebas and paramecia) that are single-celled and have varied structure and physiology and often complicated life cycles.

QUANTUM THEORY A theory in physics based on the idea that radiant energy (as light) is composed of small separate packets of energy.

RADIATION Energy radiated in the form of waves or particles.

RADIOACTIVITY The giving off of rays of energy or particles by the breaking apart of atoms of certain elements (as uranium).

SCIENTIFIC METHOD The rules and procedures for the pursuit of knowledge involving the finding and stating of a problem, the collection of facts through observation and experiment, and the making and testing of ideas that need to be proven right or wrong.

SOLUBILITY The ability of one substance, such as salt, to dissolve into another, such as water.

STEM CELL An unspecialized cell that can give rise by differentiation to a cell (as a blood cell or skin cell) with a specialized function.

SYMBIOTIC Referring to two kinds of organisms living together in close association, especially when such an association is of benefit to both (such as a fungus and an alga making up a lichen)

THERMODYNAMICS The study of the relationships between heat, other forms of energy, work, and temperature.

X-RAY Electromagnetic radiation of an extremely short wavelength that is able to move through various thicknesses of solids and to act on photographic film as light does.

INDEX

V

W

Y